LAST OF THE KNIGHTS

LAST OF THE KNIGHTS

by

JAMES A GOODSON

First Published in 1990 by
Harrop Press Ltd., 87 St Dunstan's Street,
Canterbury, Kent CT2 8AE

ISBN 1-872809-03-0

Printed in Great Britain

ACKNOWLEDGEMENTS

Without the professionalism and skills of Roger Harrop, Duncan Murray and Carol Lee of Harrop Press and particularly of Brenda Brooks, this book could not have been published.

My thanks to them all.

The incidents recorded in this book all happened, but after forty years I cannot be sure my memory is correct in every detail. I have checked with as many of the people concerned as I could reach but hope that any inaccuracies will be forgiven. Many names have been changed to avoid any possible embarrassment.

J.A.G.

CONTENTS

Prologue i

Chapter 1: Popeye . . . . Page 1

Chapter 2: Iron Crosses . . . . Page 17

Chapter 3: "Without Me" . . . . Page 42

Chapter 4: "Life is funny - and sad" . . . . Page 61

Chapter 5: Never the same again . . . . Page 76

Chapter 6: Worse than losing a Battle . . . . Page 100

Chapter 7: Illegal Entry . . . . Page 114

Chapter 8: Sentimental Journey . . . . Page 141

Chapter 9: Tears on a Row of Medal Ribbons . . . . Page 150

Chapter 10: The Last of the Knights . . . . Page 171

PROLOGUE

"I never saw a man who looked
With such a wistful eye
Upon that little tent of blue
Which prisoners call the sky".

(Oscar Wilde - The Ballad of Reading Gaol)

But my prison didn't give me even a glimpse of the sky. There were no windows in my cell and therefore no light. There was not even enough room to stretch out fully on the floor. No room, no light and now, no hope.

I needn't even have been here. It sounded like a routine mission and one I could sit out. It was to Stettin, north-east of Berlin, almost on the Baltic coast. Only one thing was a little out of the ordinary - the line showing our return route passed over Peenemunde, which we knew to be the centre of Germany's rocket reasearch. Only at the last moment, when we were at dispersal, did I decide to lead the Squadron. And only when the bombers had turned for home and I attacked the last 109 did I see something out of the corner of my eye: a short, stubby profile, a caricature of a plane hidden in a revetment on the perimeter of the airfield. As I turned, I saw it clearly. It was an Me-163 - Hitler's secret weapon.

The Me-163 was rocket powered and therefore probably twice as fast as the 262. It could be in and out of the bomber formation so fast no fighter could touch it, no gunner in the bombers would have time to fire on it. We estimated the Germans could produce 500 a month. After the first month, they would be shooting down at least 500 U.S. planes per mission, possibly doubling every month, until we lost the air supremacy on which victory depended.

I stayed in the turn. A number of thoughts flashed through my mind. I could call down the rest of the Squadron. They would be coming in above by now. But I was already down here, and I knew where the plane was. I had only used a few bursts so far and I knew I had enough ammo to take it out. Most important of all, this must be one of their few prototypes. It was a chance we'd never have again.

So far, there had been no flak, but the moment I started across the airfield it began. The bright balls of fire came sailing up, seeming to move slowly until they were close, then whizzing by. There were little black clouds of heavier flak,with exploding flashes inside them. They were mostly above me.

Automatically, I was taking evasive action, weaving and jinking, stomping one rudder and then the other, skidding and side-slipping, so that the fireballs passed beneath or behind. But I always kept my eye on the target and soon my shots were slamming into the target as I steadied the plane.

At that same moment I felt the plane shudder. I heard the crump and smelt the explosive. I felt a numbness in my right knee and knew I was hit. But it was the plane I felt for. She was like a stricken war-horse. She tried to respond, but the lifeblood was ebbing. I tried to hold her up, but as I sensed her begin to stall, I gently eased the stick forward.

Tenderly and sadly, I nursed her down, feeling her, caressing her until, as softly as I could, I let her settle on the rough ground. As we hit the ground I cut the switch. We bumped and skidded to a halt.

I slid back the hood, undid the seat harness and the 'chute and started to climb out. My right leg didn't seem to be working. I looked down. There was a lot of blood and the brown cloth of my pant leg was torn and shredded. I saw too that there was a gaping hole in the floor of the cockpit.

I hauled myself out and stood for a moment on the wing. I looked at my name and the 32 swastikas representing the official victories. I patted the side of the plane.

"Two more now, old friend! Not bad! We went out on a high note!"

There was an incendiary device to stick in the fuel tank to blow up the plane when it went down, but by now I heard and saw the rest of the Squadron coming in above me. I waved to them to shoot up old VF-B and limped off into the nearby woods. I heard the whine of the planes diving and the firing of the guns as they gave her the coup de grace. Then suddenly everything was quiet.

It was quiet now in this cell. It looked like I would be going somewhere even quieter.

I now knew that the staccato shooting I heard every morning was that of a firing-squad. I had been insisting on seeing the Kommandant. I had got as far as the "Hauptsturmfuehrer", which I learned was the SS equivalent of Captain.

"I don't care whether you are a Terror-Flieger, an escaping foreign worker, a spy or a saboteur! In any case, you are an enemy of the Reich and the Fuehrer has entrusted us with the task of eliminating all such enemies! As for the Kommandant, he is in Berlin and will not be back until tomorrow, by which time he will not have to concern himself with you. Heraus!"

Back in my cell I was no longer afraid. Then I realised that it was because my fate was inevitable that I was so calm. Fear comes from indecision as to what action to take, but it was now too late for that. The decision had been made and no action of mine could change it.

I think it was Dr. Johnson who said something like "Nothing so concentrates the mind as the knowledge that one will die on the morrow." He was right! I spent the night re-living my life - all twenty-three years of it. I thought of the strange fate that had taken me, an American, to Eurpope in 1939; placed me on the first ship to be torpedoed on the first day of the War; had me picked out of the sea and taken to England to become a volunteer fighter pilot in the RAF in those heady early months of the War. I thought of our transfer to the U.S. Air Force and my excitement when I led my Squadron of Mustangs to escort our bombers for the first time over Berlin, and later to every other target, so that finally no city, airfield or road was safe from our bombers or from our guns. And I suppose that, like the hero in a Greek tragedy, it was that feeling of power that had brought me now from those glorious heights to this sordid little death cell.

When I heard the stamp of marching feet, and the bolts crashed, and the door swung open, I was ready. I saw a tear in Hansen's blue eyes as I was marched off behind the sergeant, with two helmeted guards with sub-machine guns behind me. Not much of a funeral procession, and only a young SS guard as a mourner.

But suddenly an officer appeared, halted us, gave orders to the sergeant and led us off in a different direction. We stopped in front of a large door. It opened, and I was pushed through.

The door closed behind me. The Kommandant turned. I had always felt that Hollywood was guilty of caricaturing the real thing; but this German officer could have stepped right out of a war movie. He was a younger version of Erich von Stroheim or Conrad Veidt. From his close-cropped head to his black polished boots and in his every gesture, he was playing the part of the typical, tough SS officer. The only thing lacking was the monocle. He spoke in a high-pitched bark in an imitation of Adolf Hitler:

"I have just returned from a high-level conference in Berlin! I have decided to give you five minutes!"

I came to attention.

" As a major in the United States Army Air Force, I demand to be handed over to the Luftwaffe as a prisoner-of-war!"

"By what right?"

"By the terms of the Geneva Convention!"

Now his voice rose to a scream. "You have the nerve to mention the Geneva Convention! The enemies of the Reich have broken every rule in that Convention! As for you, you are a Terror-flieger, you are a murderer of innocent civilians, women and children! What right do you have to be treated like a soldier?"

"The same right as the men of the Luftwaffe who attacked Warsaw, Rotterdam and London!"

Thus began a most strange conversation between the man who was about to die and the man who was about to kill him. His eyes were blazing as he stared at me. I stared back. We talked about the War, about who had started the bombing, who would win the War, and why. We discussed aviation and military strategy. We discussed politics and morality and the victims of war.

Finally, perhaps realising that I was playing for time, he said "We are all victims of war, that is why I am going to have you shot!"

"I don't follow your logic, Herr Komandant. How can my death help anything? Isn't there enough death - death which can't be helped? My death would be murder. You are making a conscious decision to kill me. How can that help you? It can only cause you trouble!"

"But no, my friend, you are very clever but it won't work! However, I have enjoyed talking to you. Sit down. Would you like a drink? This is French cognac, Remy-Martin."

I sat down. "Thank you."

It was good cognac and I enjoyed it.

"I see you have a box of Cuban cigars," I said. "I always think they go well with cognac, don't you?"

He laughed, handed me the box and took one for himself.

"You are right! I, too, enjoy a good cigar!"

He struck a match, lit his cigar and threw me the matchbox. I drew deeply on the cigar, savouring it, then blew a thick round smoke-ring. Probably because I only smoked cigars, and never inhaled them, I had formed the habit of blowing rings. The air was still in the room. The ring rolled across the table and spread on the surface. The Kommandant was fascinated.

"Do that again!"

I laughed and blew another ring.

"How do you do that?"

It was one way to gain time, so I tried to teach him. He was an apt student. The session formed a bond between us. As he wrestled with the problem, he poured me another brandy.

"Thank you!" I said. "At least I'm going out in style!"

"Yes," he said, "you do have style. Prosit!" and he raised his glass.

"Is there anything else I can do for you?" he asked.

"Of course, Herr Kommandant! You could telephone the Luftwaffe!"

"No! I have no desire to make a fool of myself in front of them! I don't take orders from that lot!"

"On the contrary!" I was playing my last card. "You could be making fools of them!"

"How?" He was interested.

"You would simply say, "We are, of course, aware of the fact that a high-ranking American flying officer was recently shot down. It took you so long to find him, I thought you wouldn't mind if I mobilised my command to save further waste of time. If you wish to interrogate him, he is at your disposal. If not, I shall deal with him as I see fit!"

He continued his attempts to blow smoke rings.

"Hold it in your mouth longer before blowing it out," I suggested.

It worked. He was delighted. Then he looked at his watch, went to the telephone on his desk and barked out an order. He hung up, came back and poured us both another brandy.

When the phone rang, he swaggered over and answered it. He repeated my suggested script almost word for word. Then all I heard was a series of "Ja," "Jawohl," "Ja".

He hung up and came back to sit down with his brandy. Neither of us spoke. He proudly blew a smoke ring. Finally, he finished his drink and stood up.

"Well, it's been a long day - and night - so if you will excuse me...."

He went to the door and called for my guard, then came stiffly to attention in front of me. He shook hands, stepped back and saluted.

"Major, Leb'wohl!"

In the doorway he turned. "The Luftwaffe will pick you up in half an hour!"

I was so amazed I couldn't react. Only gradually did I realise what his words meant. I wasn't going to die. I was going to have years more of life and each year, each minute would be wonderful because it would be a precious gift.

Finally, I started to relax. I drew deeply on my cigar and blew a smoke ring.

It was perfect.

***

Chapter 1

POPEYE

I suppose we called him Popeye because of the glass eye which replaced one lost in World War I. But it was a term of respect, with no hint of ridicule, a gesture of friendship and appreciation devoid of any resentment. Other Germans were "goons", "krauts" or "bastards", nameless creatures who represented everything that was bad for us; who were responsible for our sterile lives bounded by barbed-wire fences and machinegun towers. Popeye was known to every one of the 2,000 prisoners-of-war in the Centre Compound of Stalag Luft III and he never complained if they called him Popeye instead of using his military title of "Feldwebel". He accepted it for what it was, a glimmer of affection in a hard and hostile world.

Probably only a few of the senior officers knew that his name was Strangheimer, but even they never used it, not only because they couldn't pronounce it, but because for them too he was Popeye, the one who was always there to listen to our complaints; to arrange for them to be handled as well as he could; to organise the meagre services, from the ration of strong, dark-brown Kommisbrot bread, which was the staple of our spartan diet, to the cleaning out of the latrines.

We learned very quickly that to get things done you didn't complain to the German officers - you yelled for Popeye and he always came through if he could, and above all, if it was "right". Popeye was schooled in the traditions and code of honour of the old Germany. If he ever felt that his principles and code of honour were out of place among the thousands of brash young American flying officers, he never showed it, any more than he showed any shadow of doubt about the new Nazi Germany in which he now found himself. Whatever others did or believed, Popeye knew where he stood. He was a pro.

I still remember when I first saw him.

We had spent hours locked in a third-class railway carriage on hard wooden seats, grey-uniformed guards at each end with sub-machineguns slung over their shoulders. We watched the countryside roll by on the long trip from Frankfurt to Sagan-am-Oder on the Polish border. The railway stations with the unfamiliar German names and strange lettering seemed sinister. Even the farms, the peasants, the horses and wagons, the wooden houses and barns, seemed foreign and from another, older world. As we moved East, the primitive villages made us think more of Russia than of Germany, as though we were victims of the Revolution en route to Siberia.

In the railway yards of Breslau we made one of our many long stops. A freight train moved slowly up alongside. Above the locked doors were open slots covered with barbed wire and when the train stopped we heard a strange, muted, whimpering murmur.

We looked at each other but said nothing. The guards shifted nervously and looked away from the sinister black train. We were rather relieved when we finally moved on, but the gloom was deeper and what little conversation there had been died away.

We were finally herded out onto the station platform at Sagan and marched down the road to the grim barracks, surrounded by barbed-wire fences and dominated by wooden guard towers. We were in the depths of the dumb, hopeless, lethargic depression known to all captives through the ages; the dashing aviators, the happy warriors, the be-medalled heroes, the glamour boys, the young eagles, knew they were prisoners.

It was a scruffy, unshaven, sad little group that stood before the wood and barbed-wire gate, staring at the enclosure and the wooden barracks beyond and the wooden guard towers with their grim, grey,helmeted figures behind the machineguns on the platforms.

All around was the sandy ground, with no grass, no green anywhere; only the distant black of the scrub pine beyond the triple lines of barbed-wire fencing and the rolls of barbed-wire in between.

Suddenly, the slouching guards straightened up and came to attention. A short, purposeful, erect figure was marching up. Somehow, his one eye had picked out the insignia of rank on the shoulders of my flying jacket. He came to attention in front of me, saluted smartly - with the military rather than the Nazi salute - and said "Herr Major, darf ich Sie bitten?"

I recognised this as the most correct and formal request to follow him. The German guards who had brought us here - and who had most certainly never saluted - straightened up and stood to attention under Popeye's withering one-eyed stare.

He shepherded us through the de-lousing showers, supervised the fumigation and return of our clothes and took us from the Vorlager, the reception area, to the gates of Centre Compound. Inside, the other prisoners, "Kriegsgefangenen" or "Kriegies", were waiting to greet the incoming "purge", and to ask about their squadrons and friends.

Popeye formally handed us over to the camp organisation and presented me to Colonel Del Spivey, Senior American Officer of the Centre Compound of Stalag-Luft III.

Spivey and the other officers in the camp knew all about me and were expecting me. Spivey asked me to take over as Camp Adjutant, with responsibility for all camp activities, including liaison with the German command. Serious problems were supposed to be discussed with the Lager Offizier, Major Simoleit, or even the Kommandant, Oberst von Braune. But it was Popeye who got things done.

It wasn't just the whole business of running a camp holding thousands of prisoners. It wasn't just the problems of fitting more thousands into the already-overcrowded wooden barrack blocks. In addition to the daily dramas of overflowing latrines, sudden food stoppages, physical sickness and the much worse mental illness, there were the tragedies which blotted out our rays of hope and reminded us that we were in a far and foreign land, completely at the mercy of a desperate, alien race in a war that might go on for ever.

It was like that at the ball game.

In the middle of the camp was an open area of bare ground. Here, every morning and every evening, all prisoners were assembled, drawn up according to barrack blocks, to be counted in a ceremony given the French name "appel", which the Germans had picked up in the First World War. In summer, this ground was also used for playing baseball.

It backed onto the fences. First there was the warning rail, a wire strung about a foot above the ground. About fifteen feet behind that came a tall, barbed-wire fence, and between the two were coils of barbed-wire. At each corner were the high guard towers. The machine-gunners trained their weapons down the length of the fences and had instructions to shoot if any prisoner crossed the warning wire.

The day of the ball-game was warm and sunny. Everyone was enjoying the game and the hard realities of the Kriegies life were forgotten for a little while. When the batter hit a high ball out to left field, a roar went up. Jim Atkinson was running backwards, falling back for a catch. He reached the warning wire, tripped over it and fell backwards. Immediately, the staccato burst of machineguns cut short the cheers. The crowd froze in shock.

A stocky grey figure raced to where Atkinson lay. Popeye, screaming above the rattle of the machineguns, flung himself over Atkinson's body. The shooting stopped. Popeye cradled the young officer in his arms as a mother would cradle a child. Then he slowly lifted the slight body and turned to me. All he could do was shake his head.

Taking the body to the nearest barracks, Popeye tenderly laid him down. As he turned to me, there were tears in his good eye and terrible pain in his face, but he drew himself up quickly and saluted.

"I'll make the necessary arangements, Herr Major. My deepest sympathy." And he turned on his heel.

I knew that he, too, needed sympathy, but all I could say was "Herr Feldwebel!"

He turned.

"Danke!" I said.

He never spoke English, but he must have understood a lot. He most certainly understood everything that was going on in the camp. It was Popeye, for instance, who was the first to see that Callaghan was going round the bend.

Bill Callaghan had spent months in camp, completely submerged amongst the thousands of prisoners. He was small, self-effacing and completely unnoticed. Then one day he approached me with obvious hesitation and started talking about our last theatrical production.

We had decided that, in spite of the crowded conditions, it was important to preserve one barrack block for entertainment to help morale. It also served as the reception area for new purges and for church services. Over the years, seats had been painstakingly made out of the wooden crates the Red Cross parcels came in.

The last production had been "Arsenic and Old Lace". Everyone agreed that the two fellows who played the old ladies were terrific and, for lack of volunteers, a certain Goodson had played the nephew and everyone seemed to think it was a great show. Even the Germans howled with laughter. For Callaghan, it opened up new and exciting possibilities.

"I was thinking of all the talent here in the camp, not just acting talent but musical talent!"

"Great idea!" I said. "Music is always good, and we can use the orchestra, too!"

Under the terms of the Geneva Convention, we had the equivalent of the pay of a German Officer from the Luftwaffe. The combination of low German pay levels and the low rate of exchange would have left us with almost nothing, so we pooled it to buy books for the camp library, theatrical costumes and, of course, musical instruments. Callaghan's idea was to put on a musical, made up of well-known American songs.

"Can you organise it?" I asked. "Because I don't know anyone else who could."

He said I should leave everything to him. I thought that would probably be the end of it, but during the next few weeks, I saw Callaghan everywhere, rushing from block to block, accosting the Kriegies in their constant walk around the perimeter, causing confusion by breaking the rules of the one-way traffic pattern and generally causing havoc in his increasingly frenzied activity. He was interviewing people to gather material, writing both words and music, casting and eventually producing, directing and stage-managing a mammoth epic.

Popeye first tried to alert me to what was going on. Appel had been called and the Kriegies were lined up behind their block leaders when a bearded, long-haired apparition appeared from the theatre block and sprinted to his place. After the count, Popeye saluted and reported to Major Simoleit that all were present and accounted for; Simoleit in turn saluted and repeated this information to me; I reported the same to Del Spivey and dismissed the parade - the same dull routine we went through every day. This time, however, Popeye stayed behind and it was clear he had something to say to me.

"Callaghan," he began.

"Yes?"

"Er wird verruckt!"

I smiled and agreed. In German, the word "verruckt" can mean as little or as much as the English version, crazy.

"No," said Popeye. "I mean really crazy."

"Harmless, though," I replied.

"No - we should do something!"

I shrugged. I shouldn't have.

The final rehearsals were mayhem. Callaghan was everywhere. He never stopped running; he never stopped yelling; he was never coherent. Somehow, perhaps in spite of him, the colossal production took form, having by now grown to the proportions of an Army Tattoo or a Broadway production with a cast of hundreds. Almost everyone in camp was involved, either as a source of material, as a soloist, as a member of the chorus, a player in the orchestra or as part of the army backstage.

The performance itself started with a dark and silent stage. Gradually, one became aware of the throbbing of drums and the light slowly increased to show Indians around a campfire. The songs they chanted were authentic. Callaghan had badgered the Indians in the camp to delve into their memories for the songs of their parents and grandparents. It occurred to me that most of them had probably never been written down until Callaghan did so.

After the Indians came the French explorers with their old chansons, and the colonists from all over the world with songs from their homelands. The different waves of immigration were revealed by songs from every part of Europe: the lilting songs and jigs of the Irish; the reels and pibrochs of the Scots; wild Russian dances and lively Polish polkas; the pioneers' square dances and the African chants and Negro spirituals of the slaves.

The whole panorama of American history was there in music and dance. Whole sections of the audience got up to follow their traffic pattern to the stage, whilst others rotated back to their seats. There was Country and Western and Barber Shop Quartets, George M. Cohan and "A Bicycle Built for Two", right up to the present with Glenn

Miller, Frank Sinatra, the Ink Spots and Bing Crosby.

The final scene, by contrast, was suddenly quiet and sadly familiar. It showed one of our own wooden huts, with a few prisoners lying on their bunks. From off-stage could be heard the German army songs we often heard as our guards marched by; then, in the background, another theme could gradually be heard, growing to a crescendo as it came to drown out the German songs, rising until the whole cast were singing their heads off. It was the Air Force theme song, "Off we go into the wild blue yonder."

The stage filled with virtually everyone, in various Allied Forces' uniforms. The house lights went up and those who were not on the stage joined in. The noise was deafening. It was pure corn. It was great. Even the German officers were full of praise and seemed to have overlooked the significance of the finale.

The only real casualty was Callaghan.

Even before the premiere, he had been screaming around the camp in too much of a frenzy to shave, have his hair cut or even change his clothes, but although he was getting on the nerves of the men in his barrack-block, most of the camp had observed his antics with tolerant amusement. On the day of the production, he was virtually incoherent, but we presumed he would get back to normal once the extravaganza was over.

After the show, he was more wound up than ever, but now with no outlet for his energy. He used his precious letter-forms to write to President Roosevelt and other celebrities, inviting them to a gala performance of his opus on Broadway to celebrate the end of the war. From then on, he became more and more irrational. Finally, he became violent and we decided we had to report the case to the camp Kommandant. Eventually, we were told that a psychiatrist had been called in to see him.

When the day arrived, Popeye and I accompanied Callaghan out to the Vorlager, escorted by two guards with sub-machineguns.

When we arrived outside the interview room, the psychiatrist asked Popeye and I to come in first. Callaghan had been very subdued and looked frightened as we were about to leave him with the guards. I told him we wouldn't be long, but it was Popeye's hand on his shoulder and his solemn and friendly nod that calmed him.

I gave the psychiatrist my report, and Popeye not only confirmed what I said but added so many details that it was obvious he had been keeping Callaghan under personal observation for weeks. He joined me in a plea for Callaghan to be repatriated to undergo psychiatric treatment in the United States.

That's the way it went. I'm not sure Callaghan knew what was happening, but he bade me a fond farewell, turned to Popeye and shook his hand warmly. The old sergeant stepped back, snapped to attention and saluted. The dishevelled wreck stopped snivelling and shivering, drew himself up and returned the salute. There was nothing else any man could do in response to Popeye.

As I walked back into the camp and the guards closed the gate behind me, Peter Cartwright fell into step beside me.

"How did it go with Callaghan?" he asked.

"After a few weeks of observation and treatment in a German hospital, he'll be repatriated."

"That's great!" he said.

I just looked at him and walked on.

Cartwright, sometimes called Doc, was the brains of the camp. He was one of the few who had a Ph.D. He had done a lot to build up the camp library with books brought in through the Red Cross or bought on the German market. He had also started to organise an embryo university in the form of student groups. He had worked with Callaghan on both the lyrics and music of the big show. Perhaps because of his interest in psychology, he was fascinated by the extraordinary change in Callaghan. It occurred to me that he became even more fascinated when he heard that Callaghan was being repatriated.

From then on, Cartwright became more and more active. The university expanded rapidly, thanks largely to the fact that he somehow arranged for credits from the camp to be applied to degrees in leading Universities. He was promising BA, MA and Ph.D degrees. In fact, bit by bit, step by step, he followed the rakish progress of Bill Callaghan.

Finally, he attacked a guard and, with some misgivings, we reported his condition to the German medical authorities. Once more, the little group made its way to the interview room, this time with a wild-looking Cartwright. To my surprise, he was diagnosed as being in urgent need of psychiatric treatment, to be followed by repatriation.

On the way back to camp, Cartwright was in high spirits, but Popeye was deeply sad and very serious.

"You think you are clever," he told Cartwright, "but, Herr Leutnant, you have been too clever!"

He was right. So far as I know, Callaghan was never released from a psychiatric hospital in California. Neither was Cartwright.

*****

Only a handful of escapees ever made it back from German prisoner-of-war camps, in spite of thousands of continuous attempts. Many of the desperate bids for freedom ended not only in failure, but in death; but the attempts never stopped.

Even the "Great Escape" from our camp did nothing noticeable to curtail the activities of the escape committees or of the wild independents, yet the months of minute and painstaking preparations had ended in tragedy.

They were months of digging and burrowing for everyone, with sand in the eyes, in the nose, in the mouth, in the hair. There was the constant fear of suffocation from the frequent cave-ins; the endless and dangerous task of stealing the wooden slats from the bunks and from under the barracks to shore up the constantly crumbling walls and roof of the tunnels; the boring, uncomfortable process of filling one's long underwear with sand, so that it could gradually trickle out through the ankles tied with string whilst one tramped round and round the camp perimeter, so that no trace of the newly-dug sand would be noticed by the Germans who constantly roamed the camp, searching every corner and looking for tunnels with their long metal probes.

So diversionary tunnels had to be dug, destined to be found by the goons, who would inevitably learn that there was a tunnel, but would allow it to reach a fence before breaking it in and filling it.

Then there were the monotonous service operations; the tin bashers spending their waking hours laboriously beating out the metal Klim* cans which had contained the powdered milk supplied by the Red Cross; they made all the utensils used in the camp, for the tunnels they provided the railway carts and the rails on which they travelled, carrying the sand from the face to the shaft; then there were the tailors and dyers who had to convert uniforms to civilian clothes and, through months of frustrating experiments, find materials to make the dyes in the correct colours.

The most meticulous job of all was that of the pass and document makers. In war-time Germany, all travellers, civilian or military, were constantly having their passes and travel documents checked by Military Police and Gestapo. For the fake passes, photographs had to be made with a secret and naturally forbidden camera; the right kind of paper had to be procured, and the printing reproduced under magnifying glasses, using pins to make the microscopic dots, and specially concocted inks to form letters; each individual letter could take hours. By comparison, the official Government stamps, like the stylised eagle with the swastike in its claws, were simple; they were carved from the rubber heels of flying boots.

Each of the escapers had his own fake identity with pass and documents to back it up, and most of them had learned German and rehearsed every move on their planned escape route.

But the very perfection of the operation contributed to the final tragedy. Orders went out from Berlin for the shooting of fifty of the escaped officers.

The shootings were done locally, where they were captured, usually when the car in which they were travelling was stopped to allow them to relieve themselves. They were all shot in the back of the head. One of them was Gordon Brettell who, though British, was the first commanding officer of 133 Eagle Squadron, composed of American volunteers in the RAF. It was as a result of the disastrous final mission which Brettell led, from which none of the squadron returned, that I had been transferred to 133 and, when it was eventually transferred to the US Air Force, became its C.O.

When the news of the shootings reached the camp, it was clear to the

*"Klim", is of course, milk spelt backwards!

prisoners that the Luftwaffe staff, from the Kommandant down to the lowliest goon, were deeply shocked. When the incensed Allied Senior Officers were received by the Camp Kommant, Oberst von Lindeiner, he was visibly shaken. In reply to each indignant question from the Senior British Officer, "Wings" Day, von Lindeiner could only repeat in a monotone: "I am ordered to inform you that these officers were shot whilst attempting to escape."

The British Government swore vengeance, and indeed, when the war ended, a ruthless search was made to bring to justice the Gestapo officers responsible and some men were found, tried and condemned.

At the time, the murders were considered by the Allies to be another example of senseless Nazi brutality. Brutality it certainly was, but at least from the German point of view, perhaps not so senseless. It was Popeye who gave me the first hint of it. He was too good a soldier to make any comment on the event except to offer his deepest sympathy, but we sensed his profound revulsion. It was only later that I felt I could ask him the question which bothered us so much: "Why?"

Popeye was obviously surprised. "Because they were afraid!"

Now I was the one who was surprised.

"The whole of the Third Reich afraid of fifty prisoners-of-war?"

"But of course!" he said. "Think what they could have done!"

"What?" I asked

"They could have taken the whole of Germany!"

I only understood the whole significance of what he meant when the war was over, and I was able to talk to some of those who had been responsible for the security of the Third Reich.

What emerged was an amazing picture of an administration pervaded by fear; not only fear of their superiors; not only fear of the Russian armies to the east or the Allied forces in the west; not only fear of the massive air armada pounding their country by day and by night. What terrified them more than anything else was an ever larger army right within their boundaries, within Germany's cities and towns and throughout its countryside, a desperate army filled with more hatred of Germany and its people than any armed force outside the Third Reich.

This was the army of the thousands of prisoners-of-war, the masses of slave labourers, the millions of inmates of concentration camps; an army which far outnumbered the able-bodied German males left on the home front to control them. Only one thing prevented this mighty army from overwhelming its German captors - leadership and organisation; and the Gestapo were convinced the Allies would supply both.

The escape of so many officers at one time, obviously intelligent and capable and mostly German-speaking, the very brilliance of the escape and its detailed planning confirmed their worst fears. What better way to introduce the type of officer necessary for the operation than to have them parachuted in during an air raid as air-crew? When we assured the Gestapo prisoners at Nuremberg that no such plan had been contemplated, they simply didn't believe it.

"You could have won the war in a week! You couldn't have been so stupid as not to have tried it!"

I remember thinking to myself, "But we were! we were!"

Because Popeye understood this phobia of the Nazi authorities, he pleaded with me to dissuade would-be escapers. He knew about our Escape Committee, which at least tried to limit escape attempts to those which had some slight chance of success; and as it began to look as if the war might finally end, we tended to agree with Popeye that we would be foolish to leave the relative protection of the Luftwaffe to risk the same fate as the officers in the Great Escape at the hands of the Gestapo.

The new Kommandant had signs posted, saying that escape attempts were no longer "sport". Popeye added that the old military tradition that it was the prisoner's duty to try to escape applied to the more gentlemanly wars of the past, not to the sinister, vicious, total war of Nazi Germany. Del Spivey and the other senior offices agreed that the slim chances of success, combined with the chance of the war ending soon, made escape attempts a dangerous waste of time. What's more, those precious few escapees who made it back seldom returned to active service, and were therefore more of a liability to the German state if they stayed put in a prison camp and had to be fed and guarded.

But the attempts continued; and because there was no official approval, no backing of the Escape Committee, they no longer followed the pattern of the Great Escape, with months of painstaking and meticulous preparation; instead they were desperate, sudden-death-or-glory gambles, "going for broke".

A particularly improbable attempt was made by Cassidy and Brown, who became intrigued by the comings and goings of what we called "the honey wagon".

The sanitary arrangements in the camp consisted of a series of wooden huts, known as Aborts, built at intervals around the perimeter and backing onto the forbidden no-go area in front of the barbed wire and fences. At prescribed times, the honey wagon appeared, to perform the emptying process.

This piece of equipment consisted of a large, cylindrical tank made of rubber slats, mounted on a farm wagon. On top of the tank was a large turret with a cover, through which a pipe was inserted for the purpose of filling. The pipe was connected to an engine-driven pump on the back of the apparatus by another pipe, which was lowered into the cess-pool under the Aborts.

The whole thing was driven and operated by an elderly German, familiarly known as "the honey goon". He appeared daily in one or another of the separate camps at Sagan with this horse-drawn contraption.

Both he and the horse were forlorn creatures, perhaps as a result of reflecting on the strange contribution to the German war effort that fate had called upon them to make. Their only moment of glory came when rain or snow added to the general over-loading of the facilities and the Aborts overflowed, with dramatic results. At such times, Del Spivey and I would lodge violent protests at the highest levels, the ubiquitous Popeye would swing into action and the honey wagon would appear, its driver rising to the occasion by standing up and brandishing a whip like Ben Hur; and even his sad steed seemed to respond by breaking into an accelerated shuffle.

It was this stinking contrivance that Cassidy and Brown saw as transport to freedom. On one of the honey wagon's trips to the camp, by peering through a hole at the back of the Aborts, they established the fact that the tank was only loaded to a certain level, leaving an air space in the turret. Therefore, if they could get into the tank whilst it was being filled, and if they could stand the abominable smell, they could keep their heads above the level of the liquid in the tank until the wagon had spread its loads on the fields and was left overnight.

The hare-brained scheme was thoroughly condemned by all, but the plotters were determined to go through with it.

The honey wagon duly appeared and proceeded to the Aborts. The pipe was lowered, the pump engine started, and whilst the filling was in progress, a German-speaking Kriegie offered a cigarette to the honey-goon and engaged him in conversation. At that time, cigarettes were already worth more than money and the cigarettes in the Red Cross parcels gave the prisoners a powerful weapon for bribery.

Whilst the guard was smoking his cigarette and chatting on one side of the Aborts, Cassidy and Brown crawled around the other side, clambered onto the wagon and slid through the open turret into the rising muck in the tank. When the sucking noises from the pipe indicated that the cesspool was empty, the guard stopped the engine, coiled up his pipes, slammed the cover on the turret and drove off.

The camp activities continued as normal, but every eye was on the wagon as it trundled towards the main gate of the camp. Before it reached the barrier, however, a horrified expression on the face of the driver signified that all was not well. From the wooden tank came sounds of banging, and muffled shouts. The honey goon pulled up his horse, clambered back to the turret and threw it open.

Two reeking figures, covered in slime from head to foot, were dragged gasping and choking from the tank.

They had failed to take into account the sloshing effect of the load as the wagon lurched and jolted on its way and wave after wave filled the precious air pocket in the turret. They had held out until they were close to drowning before pounding on the turret cover.

Popeye was both amazed and horrified by this escapade and asked if I could explain such foolhardiness.

"Never underestimate the urge for freedom," I said. "Give me liberty or give me death!"

He shook his head sadly.

"Wer ist heute frei? Who is free today?"

Popeye felt strongly that we were fortunate to be protected from the harsh realities of war.

"For you, the war is already over," he said. "You are lucky!"

He was ready to do his patriotic duty to his Fatherland, as he had in World War I, but he considered himself also to be lucky, to be at the camp instead of at the Front.

But as the end of World War II approached in Germany, nobody was safe. One day, there was a different sergeant doing the counting on parade.

"Where's Strangheimer?" I asked Major Simoleit.

"Compassionate leave. His home in Westphalia was bombed."

"Is his family alright?"

"All dead."

I was stunned.

"All dead?"

Simoleit shrugged. "That's war," he said.

He was clearly as shocked as the rest of us and it was then I realised for the first time that every Kriegie in the camp knew Popeye. Most had been helped by him at some time; all respected him. Maybe part of the profound sadness was because many of them now saw the individual tragedies which were caused when they activated the toggle-switch and released the load of bombs, the personal grief behind the smoke puffs far below.

After they had absorbed the news, both individual Kriegies and block leaders representing their barracks came to me with the same question: "Can't we do something?"

But what could aircrew prisoners-of-war do, or say? Nothing.

It was when Nick Nagurka came to me that I got an idea. Nick was a leading light of the camp orchestra.

"Nick, have you ever heard of a piece of music called the Westfalen Lied?"

"No," he said. "What is it?"

"It's a sort of national anthem of the State of Westphalia and it's beautiful. I'll get the music for you - they must have it in the Kommandantur, or be able to get it."

"What for?" asked Nick.

"Popeye comes from Westphalia."

After ten days, Popeye returned from leave. We were drawn up on parade for Appel, an unusually silent Appel; the two thousand officers stood stock still as Colonel Spivey, the German Lager Offizier and myself waited for Popeye and his men to complete the count. It was over sooner than usual, and we went through the usual routine of Popeye reporting "Alles in Ordnung", Major Simoleit repeating it to me and me to Del Spivey. But instead of Del then giving me permission to dismiss the parade, I turned back to face the officers, called them to attention and turned to Popeye.

"Herr Feldwebel," I began in German, "every prisoner in this camp wishes to express his deepest sympathy, in the only way we can."

I turned back to the lines of officers.

"Parade! Present arms!"

Every officer saluted and held it, whilst the sorrowful strains of the Westfalen Lied floated out over the still camp.

They say that people with a glass eye only shed tears with their good eye. It isn't true. They both weep.

****

Chapter 2

IRON CROSSES

Outside the world of Stalag Luft III, more historic events were reaching their climax. In one of the barracks we had drawn a great map of Europe on the wall, and as the Russian armies moved westward towards us, a line of red string supported by pins was moved forward as we heard of one obscure Russian town after another being fought over.

The only news we were allowed was the OKW (Oberkommando der Wehrmacht) official German military announcements piped to us over loudspeakers, and strangely enough they gave amazingly accurate information of where the fighting was taking place. They may have realised the Russian or Polish areas referred to meant nothing to the average German. We, however, had maps in the camp library and the time to study them. The German officers and goons would look at our map and were always shocked or incredulous when they saw how close the line was coming.

But of course, we did get the BBC news every evening, even though the Germans never ceased to search for the clandestine radio. They never knew that I was telling the truth when I told them no such radio existed, for it only came into being for the time of the evening broadcast, and then disappeared. Just before the given time, observers were discreetly posted to warn of the approach of any goon. A minute before zero hour, several Kriegies would converge on one spot. By the number, each man would produce one component of the set, and in seconds the receiver was assembled and the shorthand artists began to take down the message, which would later be passed to every PoW in the block. In case of danger, it could be disassembled just as fast. This masterpiece of organisation was perfected in every compound of the camp and, so far as I know, none of them were ever found.

But the day came when we needed no radio, German or English, to tell us the news. We could actually hear the distant crump of artillery to the North-East. Stalag-Luft III was on the River Oder at Sagan, close to the Polish border, south-east of Berlin and north of Breslau.

After Appel, I asked Popeye what he thought would happen. After all, if the Russians could not be stopped at the Oder, they could not be stopped until they reached Berlin. The war had to be over. At least there would be no point in transporting thousands of prisoners-of-war even deeper into Germany.

But Popeye understood the thinking of the German High Command better than that. He knew that no-one, from Hitler down, would dare to think, let alone speak, about defeat.

"If they cross the Oder," said Popeye, "we'll be ordered to move you out of this area."

The colonels held a Council of War to decide what to do if we were marched out of Sagan. Knowing that the Russian armies were within a few miles of us, many prisoners would want to make a break for it rather than be marched off to another prison camp to probable worse captivity, or even death.

After much soul-searching, we agreed with Del Spivey that mass escapes would provoke a violent reaction, probably ending in a blood bath. There seemed to be no way in which the Germans could mount a counter-offensive to stop the inexorable advance of the Russians from the East, the Allies from the West and South and the relentless bombing and strafing from above. The thought of a man surviving combat and enduring months of captivity, only to be killed a few months, weeks or even days before the end of the war, was uppermost in our minds. As for the possible danger awaiting us in further captivity, time enough to react to that when it happened.

Another consideration was the question of Russian reaction. Reports trickling through to us indicated that they shot first and asked questions later. What's more, they had been advancing so fast that organisation and control had almost broken down. Almost certainly, in the utter confusion and chaos following in the wake of a conquering army, there would be no machinery for repatriating Allied prisoners-of-war, or even for taking care of them.

In the event, there was little chance of escape. At the same time that the Lager Offizier announced that the Russians had crossed the Oder to the north of us, the compound filled with German guards with sub-machine guns, shouting "Raus! Raus! Alle Raus!" The Hund-fuehrers were there with their barking, snarling Alsatian dogs straining at their leashes. We were given a short time to collect the few possessions we could carry with us.

When the bedraggled columns were lined up, they looked like refugees look in every country and in every age. The straight-backed, bright-eyed, flashy young Air Force officers were now miserable, bent figures, huddling together in the freezing wind. Instead of parade-ground uniforms, they were bundled up in a drab collection of khaki coats, slacks, sweaters, leather flying jackets and old uniform tunics. Some had scarves wrapped around their heads, either under or over old officer's caps, and all were festooned with bags containing the few personal treasures they were allowed to take with them. A few carried their cooking utensils, made out of beaten Klim cans.

Along the lines of prisoners were the German guards, menacing with their sub-machine guns and straining, snarling dogs. They were obviously nervous, and therefore dangerous. I told the German officers to calm them down, but when a guard got too aggressive the prisoners looked to Popeye, and Popeye was always there.

The Germans were afraid that when the order was given to move off, the prisoners would simply refuse to move. Maybe it was the advice of the Senior Officers that this was not the time to provoke a confrontation that prevented the electric tension from exploding. In any case, there was the added persuasion of a sinister-looking machine pistol prodding you in the back. Under those circumstances, when they shout "Marsch!" you marsch.

The long lines shuffled off through the ice and wind and drifting snow. Popeye and I went to the Vorlager where the Red Cross parcels were stored. The artillery was getting closer now and we heard not only the crump of the firing, but the whistle of the shells and the sharper cracks as they landed. The German camp was all confusion. Apparently they had had no more warning than we had.

But in the little office in front of the warehouse, all was normal. Popeye told the sergeant he had horses and wagons outside to transport the Red Cross parcels which the prisoners would need on the march. He handed him a chit signed by Colonel Spivey and by the Camp Kommandant, Oberst von Braune.

The German Feldwebel was short and balding. He sat behind a wooden counter, in front of the locked doors that led to the warehouse. He looked sceptically at the chit through his rimless glasses, and shook his head.

"This chit is no good to me. You know perfectly well it requires a form 13801-B signed by each Lager Offizier before I release a single crate."

The shelling got louder. Now we could hear small-arms fire.

"Do you mean you want to leave all this for the Russians and let our people starve?" Popeye asked him incredulously.

"I know my orders," and he continued writing figures in his ledger.

Popeye went to the door and called in his men from outside. The Warehouse sergeant said, "I won't unlock the door."

A nod from Popeye and his men were battering the door open with the butts of their rifles and machine pistols. The Warehouse sergeant was threatening to bring the full, awful power of the entire Luftwaffe down on Popeye and all his men.

When the door was open, Popeye ordered his men to load. He did make one concession. The Warehouse sergeant insisted on noting the number of each crate in his ledger, and Popeye had each man call out the number as each crate was carried out. This inevitably delayed the whole procedure.

As the shelling got closer, I began to wonder how the camp was getting on and whether I shouldn't be with them, rather than loading Red Cross parcels.

"Can't we forget checking the numbers?"

Popeye shrugged. "He's right, you know."

Finally, all was loaded, checked and signed for. Outside, the noise and confusion was growing. Popeye asked the sergeant, "Are you coming with us?"

"Oh no," he said. "There are other goods. My place is here."

Popeye snapped to attention and saluted. The sergeant did the same, then sat down behind his desk, took his pistol from its holster, laid it on the desk in front of him and went back to writing in his ledger.

"He's nuts!" I said.

"He's a soldier," said Popeye.

I thought it would take a long time to catch up with our compound, but as we watched the refugees and even the German soldiers stumbling through the snow, slipping on the ice and staggering into the drifts on the side of the road to let our horses and wagons pass, we realised that the march would be slower and tougher than we had imagined. When we caught up with the rear end of our compound, we saw that there was another factor.

Although many of the prisoners had tried to keep in good physical shape, others, known as "sack artists", had spent most of their time in their bunks, reading, snoozing or day-dreaming. These were now unable to keep up. They were floundering in the snow, while the guards prodded them with their guns and threatened to shoot them.

Without a word, Popeye and I leapt down from the wagon. We pulled the guards back and lifted the exhausted Kriegies to their feet. Those in worst shape we loaded onto the wagons. The others we half carried, half dragged along until we caught up with the main body.

But the whole camp had slowed down. It wasn't only the snow and ice. It wasn't only the exhaustion. There was above all the pathetic stream of refugees; there were the retreating rear echelon administration troops of the German armed forces, whose vehicles slithered to a halt and blocked the roads; there were other prisoners-of-war and slave labourers of every nationality and, above all, the Polish refugees, trying to carry what was left of their precious possessions on broken-down carts and wagons.

Most of them seemed to be farmers. Their wagons were piled high with furniture, utensils, farm implements and other equipment imaginable and unimaginable, useful and useless. Both male and female members of the family led the floundering horses and cattle and helped push the lurching wagons. As often as not, the women and youngsters were dragged along until they regained their feet or fell into the snow. Many had to be left behind, particularly the old and weak.

As we stumbled past one group of refugees who had stopped at the side of the road, their leader came up to me. Although he spoke in Polish, I understood enough to know that he wanted a doctor. We did not have one among the Kriegies, so I asked Popeye to send a guard for a German doctor.

Popeye and I followed the Polish peasant around to the other side of his wagon. There, only partly sheltered by other members of the family, was a young woman obviously in the throes of childbirth. The older woman who was trying to cope with the situation looked up at me. Since I had been brought there by the head of the family, she presumed I was a doctor and quickly turned her responsibilities over to me. I turned to Popeye.

"Do you know anything about these things?"

"I had to help out when our first was born."

"Move in!" I said.

The woman was alternately moaning and screaming. Her agony was real and I knew something was very wrong. Popeye made his examination.

"Breech birth," he said.

I didn't understand.

"Back to front," he said, and added the gesture.

"What do we do?" I asked.

"Turn it around," he replied.

I'd always known childbirth meant pain. Now I learned it meant violent, exhausting physical effort. It wasn't a blessed event in my view, it was a bloody mess.

Somehow, when hope and strength were almost gone, it happened. At the moment of birth, the German doctor appeared. We staggered to our feet and left him to it, but Popeye was still calling the shots.

"Schnapps!" he yelled.

Almost immediately, one of the Poles produced a bottle. Popeye dropped down beside the young mother, who was showing no sign of life, forced her mouth open and tipped up the bottle. She spluttered and gasped - and breathed. Popeye handed me the bottle and I helped myself, then handed it back to him. Then the doctor held out his hand, but he didn't want it for himself. He used it as an antiseptic. The Poles obviously considered this a waste of good schnapps.

As soon as the doctor had finished, the Poles were anxious to move on. The young mother was helped to her feet, led to a wagon slightly less over-loaded than the others, and lifted onto it. To the crack of whips and encouraging shouts, the wagons lurched off. The new mother, cradling her baby, waved to us.

"Tough people, the Poles," I said.

Popeye nodded.

As Popeye and I trudged after our Compound, the short winter day was ending. The temperature dropped even lower and the wind blew stronger. We passed more and more figures collapsed in the snow by the roadside, unable to walk any further.

"They'll freeze to death tonight," I said. Popeye nodded.

When we reached the end of our own group, the guards were prodding the last prisoners to make them keep up. There were more of them riding on the wagons carrying the Red Cross crates, and many were hanging onto the sides. The guards explained that the officers were worried because the pace had slowed and they had orders to get us out of the front line area as soon as possible.

Presumably with the same thought in mind, the Kommandant informed Del Spivey that all senior officers would be separated from the rest and taken on ahead by train. Spivey called me aside and entrusted me, as Camp Adjutant, with the responsibility of Senior Officer.

"I know you'll try to keep discipline, Jim, but it wouldn't take much for the guards to panic and start shooting. A handful of German guards are trying to control thousands of able-bodied young officers, with thousands of well-armed Russians advancing on them fast. The Kriegies know that, too, and most of them will want to escape. If they do, that's all it will take for this march to turn into a bloodbath. Even those that escape the guards could get shot by the German front-line troops - or even the Russians. Your only hope is to keep everyone together, so the guards don't panic. Above all, don't let anyone try to escape. That would trigger off a catastrophe."

"Del," I said, "I know you're right. It would be a tragedy if any of our men lost their lives after surviving right up to the end. I agree that the Germans are desperate and might do anything. But in spite of all that, I don't feel I can order them not to try to escape. I'll give them all the arguments against it, and advise against it, but if, in spite of everything, they still want to go, I can't order them not to."

I was thinking of millions of miserable creatures in concentration camps and prison camps throughout Germany, dumbly submitting to their fate until they lost all spirit and pride and became like senseless broken beasts. Maybe it was inevitable and even sensible that a human being should accept captivity rather than risk death, but I would never order it.

Del Spivey understood. We'd often spoken of it before.

"Okay Jim, but for God's sake, don't you go. They all depend on you!"

We had reached one of the few isolated villages. Beyond the village was miles of open space with no protection. It was obvious to me that if we were forced to keep going we would lose a lot of men. I knew that Popeye agreed, but there was nothing he could do.

We had to make a stand now if the whole operation was to be kept under control, preferably our control. I found Major Simoleit, the German officer who had been left with us, who immediately launched into a tirade to the effect that we had to keep going or be shot.

"Herr Major", I said, "in that case, since we risk getting shot anyway, I will immediately give orders to all our officers to escape. Our Allies, the Russians, are a few kilometres away. Your guards will shoot some of us, but most of us will get away. You know what the reaction of the German High Command would be, and who would be held responsible?"

For almost a minute we confronted one another, looking straight into each other's eyes. Simoleit wavered first. He knew I was right. He turned to Popeye.

"Guard this officer!" and to me, he said, "If one prisoner escapes, you will be shot!"

The stop gave us time to bring up the stragglers. It gave the rest time to flop down and eat and sleep. We brought up the Red Cross wagons. Although the guards had had nothing to eat all day, not one crate was missing. They had defended them from starving refugees and even German soldiers. Popeye and I ran around like mother hens.

More important than the distribution of Red Cross parcels was the problem of shelter for the night from the bitter cold. We were in Upper Silesia, a sparsely populated farm area. There was little protection from the icy blasts which seemed to be coming straight from the Arctic.

The little village was really just a collection of houses and farm buildings along the road, with a church in the middle. It's name was Seligesruhe, Blessed Rest.

"Hier nehmen wir unsere Seligesruhe", I told the Kommandant. "Here is where we take our blessed rest!"

He shrugged and left. I turned to Popeye.

"We're sleeping here, but not in the open."

He looked startled. "Then where?"

I pointed to the little houses lining the road.

"There," I said, "and there", pointing to the church.

"Impossible!" he said. "Possibly in the barns, but not in the houses, and certainly not in the church!"

"Yes, we'll use the barns, if there's enough hay in them, but we'll still need to put some officers in the houses and in the church."

"We couldn't guard all the houses!"

"On the contrary, you can guard them better. Anyone who strays from the building, you shoot, just like in the camp. Also, if they stay outside in the snow they will freeze to death - and I'm not going to let them freeze to death."

"But the peasants would never accept enemy soldiers in their houses. They'd be terrified. And as for the House of God..."

"You handle the peasants," I said, "and I'll handle God."

He looked at me hard. He knew that if anything went wrong it was he, not I, who would be shot. He wanted to make sure that I knew it, too.

"Can you give me your word that no officer will try to escape, and that no harm of any kind will come to the church, or the houses, or the people in them?"

"That no-one will try to escape, no. That no harm will come to the church, houses and people, yes."

We went down the main street together, knocking at each door and allocating to each little house a small group of those prisoners who were in the worst physical shape. Most of the cottages had only women in them. As in most of Germany, the men were away in the armed forces. We explained, with more conviction than we felt, that these dishevelled, unshaven tramps were officers and gentlemen and that they had nothing to fear. Furthermore, they would stay in the front room only, leaving the rest of the house to the owners. We explained the same thing to the officers and gentlemen, and added a few dire threats of mine.

When the front room of each house and cottage was filled, we moved on to the church. It was large for the size of the village and we fitted more than a thousand men into it. When it was full, I mounted the stairs to the pulpit.

While I waited for the mock applause and crude jokes to die down, I looked around at the memorial slabs, and particularly at the big black board which carried the names of the dead of both world wars. It reminded me of the war memorials in small villages in England, where there seemed to be more names than there were inhabitants in the village, and every family name appeared at least once. Here, in the church of Seligesruhe, many of the names had an Iron Cross hanging on a nail beside them.

When the noise had died down, I made my brief speech.

"This is the house of God. I have given my word that you will not desecrate it. If you do, the lucky ones will be dealt with by God, who will consign their souls to everlasting hell. The less fortunate ones will be dealt with by me."

We went off to fill the barns and sheds. It was January, so there wasn't much hay left, but we gathered it together and soon everyone was taken care of for the night.

It was getting dark. Outside the barns, outside the church, in front of the houses, little lights flickered as the Kriegies lit their Klim can stoves. One tin can had openings in the sides for draught. Into this went the wood shavings which were lit, blown upon and coaxed into flame. When it was burning, another can full of water was placed on top. Soon the water was boiling, the Nescafe was put in and the coffee made. At the same time, slices of heavy black army "kommis brot" were pressed to the hot sides of the bottom can to be toasted.

The Red Cross parcels were distributed by the goons as efficiently as in the camp. Popeye posted his guards.

"We can't do anything more," I said. "You are tired - go get some sleep. Gute Nacht, und danke!"

"I can't. I have to guard you," he said in a sad and weary voice.

"No, you don't. Schlafen Sie gut!"

I looked deep into his one grey eye and smiled. He slowly smiled back and saluted.

"Gute Nacht, Herr Major, und danke!"

When I returned to the main street, a few men were waiting to see me.

"We want to go over the hill," they said. "In this confusion, we could evade the guards and hide up until the Russians come through."

"So when are you leaving?" I asked.

"Tonight!"

I shrugged. "The village is surrounded by open fields covered with snow. The guards have it covered and will spray everything that moves. You won't stand much of a chance against that background. Why not wait until we're on the move again tomorrow, when you can mingle with the refugees and slip away in the general confusion? Besides, we've persuaded Popeye to let us sleep inside tonight. If, as a result, there's an escape, he's had it."

"You mean they'd shoot him?" someone asked.

"For sure," I said.

"And you?"

"Probably," I said, and walked off to find somewhere to bed down. Jim Devinney materialised.

"For God's sake, come on!" he said. "We've got a reserved seat for you!"

I followed him down the main street, through a picket gate into a snow-filled front garden and up to a small farm cottage. When we opened the door, we found ourselves in a well-lit front parlour. It was warm, thanks to an old-fashioned iron stove set in an old fireplace. Seated on either side of it were an old woman dressed in black and huddled in a shawl, a middle-aged woman wearing a faded apron over her woollen dress and a younger woman wearing a kerchief on her head, a rough dress with men's trousers beneath it and heavy boots. She had obviously been working in the farm buildings behind the house. Around the room, sitting on the floor with their backs to the wall were eight prisoners. On a table was an old radio.

I was solemnly introduced to the three women. The grandmother was a widow from the First World War. The middle-aged woman was her daughter, and the younger woman the wife of her son. There had been some children, who had apparently been evacuated. Both women's husbands were "at the Front", somewhere in the East. They had had no news for some months, and the constant rumble of the guns must have reminded them that the "Front" was now almost in their back garden.

The Kriegies had shared their Red Cross parcel with them. They had eaten the hard chocolate but had carefully kept the pack of cigarettes. I wondered idly who would finally smoke those Lucky Strikes; certainly not their own menfolk - probably the Russians.

The young woman gave me some kommis brot and a hot sausage. Jim passed me a can of coffee from the stove.

"May I suggest that this Chateau Lafitte '28 would go well with your T-bone steak, sir?"

"No, send it to the servants' quarters," I said. "I've been so spoiled by the rich food and drink lavished upon me by the Third Reich, I'd give anything for a simple sausage and a cup of coffee!"

And it was almost true. Even looking back today, the memory of that Silesian farm sausage and black bread rates higher than that of dinners at Maxims and the Savoy Grill.

"Did you ever think of how much misery could have been turned to pleasure in the last fifty years, if the Germans had stuck to making sausages instead of war? People should do the things they do best."

"That's what I always say to my girlfriends," said Jim. "Let's do the things I do best!"

The old lady sighed, "Ja, ja," and nodded her head. It was a sigh of resignation and ineffable sadness. "Ja, ja."

Over the radio came the first few bars of "Deutschland, Deutschland, Uber Alles," which always preceded the news. "Der Oberkommando der Wehrmacht gibt bekannt," said the announcer.

Then came the usual story of heroic defence by German front-line troops obeying the Fuehrer's order to stand firm, but the names of the small areas and towns where the fighting was going on were familiar to us from studying the maps, and we knew they were not far away. There was the usual quotation of rousing words from the Fuehrer and Goebbels, and the announcement of "Terror" air-raids and the number of Allied aircraft shot down.

But it was the last quiet announcement that meant the most: "Hiermit beendet sich die Sendungen Ober-Schlesien. Gute Nacht!" - (Radio Silesia now ends its broadcasting. Good night.) So the Russians were at Frankfurt-am-Oder.

The sad strains of "Deutschland Uber Alles" again came over the air and then suddenly and finally stopped.

"Ja, ja," sighed the old lady.

The next morning I was awakened by a great commotion. Popeye was storming into the room asking for me. My first thought was that the would-be escapees had made a break during the night, but the look in Popeye's eye told me it was worse than that.

He asked me to follow him to the church. He led me through the half-awakening bodies to the War Memorial and pointed. At first I could see nothing wrong; but then I understood. The black-ribboned Iron Crosses beside the names had all gone. Only the bare nails remained.

I mounted the steps to the pulpit and roared at the confused multitude. I can't remember what I bellowed in my anger. Certainly such blasphemous profanity had never been heard before in that House of God. I told the culprits they had been guilty of the foulest of sins, that their parents, children and grandchildren would be branded by the shame of this deed, that because of them the Air Force, their country and their comrades, dead and alive, would disown them. When I stopped for breath, there was a deathly silence.

Quietly, I said, "I'm leaving this church now. I will be back in 2 minutes and I expect to see every one of those crosses back in its place."

Popeye and I left and walked a few yards up the street.

"It seems even colder," I said to Popeye.

"Yes," he said. "Last night was bad - most of our guards got frost-bite."

I turned to go back into the church. He put his hand on my arm.

"Please give them five minutes, Herr Major."

The church was emptying fast when we got back. We went straight to the board and looked up. Every Iron Cross was back on its nail.

"Thank you!" he said.

"Thank God!" I murmured.

When the unwieldy trek began again, we again had the task of keeping the marchers together as the difference between the fit and the unfit became even more obvious. I demanded to know how long the march had to continue and where we were going. But it was obvious that the Germans were as much in the dark as we were. I told them that we would continue to the next town with rail connections, but no further. They said they were expecting orders any minute, but in the meantime we had to keep moving as fast as possible. Apparently, the front line was getting closer to us all the time.

As we stumbled and slithered along, we again encountered the family of Polish refugees we had met the day before. The young mother was walking alongside the wagon now, one hand ready to steady her baby, which was sleeping among the goods and chattels in the cart in spite of the jolting and lurching. Some of our Polish speakers were trying to talk with them. I asked them to try to find out why the refugees were leaving their farms in Poland instead of waiting for the Russians to arrive. Their reply was the same I had heard from Poles in the RAF and from Mike Sobanski.

"For centuries, we have been attacked and invaded by the Russians from the East and the Germans from the West. We hate them both, but of the two, we prefer the Germans by far."

They told us of scenes of pillage, murder and rape as an undisciplined Russian army made its way through Poland, but before we could check whether these were eye-witness accounts or simply rumours, the German guards broke it up and the Poles were forced to move aside to let us through.

We plodded on through groups of refugees, other prisoners, and other German units.

Then we found ourselves moving through a different group, white camouflaged troops. They were lying in the snow, motionless and silent. Ahead of us, we saw what looked like a statue. As we got closer, we saw it was a horse. Standing on its back was an officer in German uniform wearing a Cossack hat, looking over the troops through a pair of binoculars. I was at the head of the column behind a small group of German officers and NCOs. They obviously wanted to know what the officer was looking at. As I came up, Major Simoleit asked if I could speak Russian.

"Why do you ask?"

"This is Vlassov's army, and we want to ask the officer how close the front is, but he hardly speaks any German."

I had heard of General Vlassov, the Russian who had defected to the Germans with most of his army and had added to it since. I only knew a few words of Russian, but as soon as the officer understood that I was American, he asked, "Est-ce vous parlez Francais?"

I was amazed. The probability of one of the few Russian officers able to speak French meeting a French-speaking American officer on the German front must have been wildly remote.

His French was not good, but most enthusiastic, and he was delighted to meet an American. He leapt down from his horse, embraced me and kissed me on both cheeks. I must have showed my surprise by recoiling a bit. He immediately stepped back and saluted. He had thin, almost aristocratic features, rather than the normal Slavic face of most Russians. He looked and played the part of the typical Cossack.

"Ask him how close the enemy forces are," said Simoleit.

"Venez! I'll show you!" he shouted.

He mounted his horse and plunged into the snow, waving for us to follow him. I didn't hesitate, in case the German officers and guards should stop me. I floundered after the Cossack officer, with Simoleit and a couple of guards after me.

He led us to a small wood. As we entered it, we saw that it was full of horses and men. The officer shouted to them in Russian and they mounted up. We went on through the trees to the other side. In front of us was a snow-covered hill sloping down into a valley with a frozen river at the bottom. On the other side of the river, the ground rose again, covered with trees.

As we reached the far edge of the wood, we saw in front of us more men lying in the snow, pointing their machine pistols over what looked like sandbags, which they were using as cover. When we looked closer, we saw that the sandbags were horses, lying flat on the snow in front of their riders.

The officer pointed down to the frozen river. We could see the Russian infantry emerging from the trees and beginning to cross. In front of them was the open space of the hill, at the top of which was the main road along which we had been marching. The wood where we stood was like a tongue protruding down the hill.

The Russian officer explained his simple strategy.

"They have been ordered to cut the road and make a pincer movement.

They are being pushed forward fast, ahead of the tanks, which are probably short of gasoline, and anyway can't operate well in those trees. They will go straight for the road, which they can see, crowded with refugees. We will surprise them with our little pincer movement."

I was surprised by his enthusiasm and the discipline of his men.

"But why do you fight with the Germans against Russia?" I asked.

"We don't fight against Russia; we fight FOR Russia!" he shouted. "We fight the murderers and cowardly bureaucrats who have taken over our beloved country. All decent Russians want to throw them out, but we have the courage to seize this opportunity. It is our last chance. If this fails, we will be slaves for the rest of our lives, and our children and grandchildren, too!"

"But how can you fight for the Nazis, the enemies of freedom and decency and democracy?"

"We don't fight for them, we fight with them. Of course we'd rather fight with you, but you are so naive. You can't see that your real enemy is the Bolsheviki!"

"But Hitler is a criminal and a murderer."

"Ha!" he laughed, "and Stalin is a choir-boy!"

"But there's no freedom under the Nazis."

"My innocent friend, I can tell you the biggest prison in the world is the Soviet Union!"

"But what will happen to you when the Germans lose the war?"

He shrugged. "Maybe we fight with you against the Bolsheviks. Maybe we fight with the Russian people against the bureaucrats. Maybe we fight alone. But at least we will have fought, and if we lose, it will be better than never having fought at all. This is our last chance."

Then he laughed. "Nous sommes la Légion maudite! - We are the Legion of the Damned!"

The Russian troops were coming up the hill now. The officer mounted his horse and went back into the wood. Soon the Russian infantry would see the defending soldiers in the snow.

Suddenly, the whole scene erupted. The white camouflaged troops on the German side started shooting. The attacking Russians started running towards them, firing as they ran. They dropped to the ground when they were close to the defenders and waited for more troops to come forward. They came up in scattered groups, with no apparent organisation.

When the Russians seemed to be stopped, at least temporarily, shouts and what sounded like rebel yells broke out from the wood, and the cavalry came galloping out. The other horses which had been lying on the snow lunged up onto their feet, their riders already in the saddle, and joined in the wild charge. The officers were waving swords, but the other Cossacks were firing submachine guns. As they got closer to the enemy, the horses kept their heads lower and lower as the bullets whistled over their ears. There was even a sleigh or troika in the midst of the melée, a machine-gunner in the back and another soldier feeding in the belt. When they got into the thick of things, they hurled grenades into the enemy troops.

The charge never slowed down. They sliced through the enemy, gunning them down, putting the rest to flight, pursuing them and then wheeling back. In the meantime, the white-camouflaged infantry had emerged from the snow and followed the cavalry, mopping up what was left of the Russians and advancing after those who were retreating before the wild Cossack charge.

The Russian troops retreated across the river and into the protection of the woods on the slopes oppposite. The German infantry threw themselves down in the snow and the Cossack cavalry swung round behind them, some disappearing into the woods, other dismounting and crouching down again in the snow.

The German officers turned to go back to the march, indicating to the guards to bring me along. I looked back and saw the Cossack officer on his horse looking after us. I waved. He waved back; a slow wave, a sad wave, which ended in a military salute.

The Germans were obviously shocked at having seen the Russian troops so close. They knew that what we had seen was just a holding action, and that the Russians only needed to wait for more troops, tanks and artillery to catch up, and their advance would continue like a great juggernaut.

Major Simoleit came to me and told me we must speed up the march to get out of the combat area.

"Impossible!" I said. "Look at the stragglers we have already! Even your guards are having trouble keeping up. There's only one thing to do - head for the nearest railway station and get us onto a train. This aimless marching is getting us nowhere!"

He assured me that everything was under control and that he was awaiting orders from headquarters.

"You'd better tell headquarters to get the trains to the nearest town, because we won't go any further!"

My arguments were underlined when Popeye came up, saluted and reported that some officers were missing. He had handled the problem of counting us by having his guards stand on the side of the road as we marched by. It must have been amazingly accurate, because they had the number right.

"Ten officers missing!" shouted Simoleit. "This must stop!"

"No, Herr Major," I replied. "Each day there will be more, as long as we are kept marching. I suggest you tell that to your headquarters."

"They will be shot, either by my guards, or the Gestapo, or the Russians!"

"If the march continues, they will die of exhaustion and cold."

Simoleit playing the tough disciplinarian was out of character. He looked at me, saw that I meant it, and shrugged his shoulders with typical Austrian resignation.

"You will march to the nearest town. I will make sure rail transport is made available."

"How far is the next town?" I asked.

"We can make it by tonight if we keep going," replied Simoleit.

"We MUST make it by tonight!" I told him. What's it called?"

"Muskau!"

In German, it was pronounced "Moscow". When he saw the look on our faces, he showed us his map. It was further than we had thought. We figured the main group of marchers could make it, but the number of stragglers had been increasing all the time and some of them were in bad shape. It wasn't just the festering blisters on the feet; there was dysentery and 'flu and frostbite; all the minor ailments, too, that could be expected among hundreds of men.

Nevertheless, we had to do our best. I said I'd bring on the stragglers as fast as I could. Popeye volunteered to accompany me. At the end of the ragged column, we found larger and larger gaps. The straggling marchers stumbled along with a glazed look in their eyes and a vacant look on their faces. The Germans guards marched alongside, goading them on and, when they faltered, prodding them with their guns.

Behind came the horses and wagons, originally loaded with Red Cross parcels, now overloaded with prisoners who had fallen and couldn't walk any further. Other marchers clung to the sides to help themselves along. When one of the flagging marchers dropped and couldn't be revived, the guards threw him on to one of the wagons, but because the wagons were already loaded to the limit, they had to throw off one of the others to stumble along as best he could. I saw that this couldn't go on. Sooner or later one of them would drop and either be left to die in the snow or be shot by one of the guards. They had orders to leave no-one behind. I turned to Popeye.

"This can't go on! These are American officers! Tell your men to treat them as such! We may not get to Muskau as soon as the others, but we'll get there - all of us!"

Popeye sprang into action. The wagons were stopped whilst we inspected all the PoWs and selected those who couldn't walk at all. We piled the remaining Red Cross crates onto one wagon and sent it ahead to distribute them amongst the other marchers and then return. Then we separated the "wounded" into those who would ride in the wagons, those who would take turns riding and those who would have to walk, but at a slower pace.

As we painfully plodded along, we picked up other stragglers from the front column of marchers and accomodated them as best we could.

A large group of German guards had been allotted to bring up the rear of the column, to make sure no-one lagged behind and with strict orders to shoot those who couldn't keep up. But now, under the watchful eyes of Popeye and myself, they willingly changed their attitude. Most of them were over 50 and had been invalided out of front-line duty as a result of war wounds; but in spite of little food and less sleep, they kept going with no sign of weakening. They helped to push the over-loaded wagons, went to the aid of those who staggered and fell, and even supported and half-carried the weakest. All this with their automatic rifles slung over their shoulders.

I suggested to Popeye that they share our Red Cross parcels, but he dismissed such a breach of discipline out of hand. Even when we doled out bits of chocolate to the PoWs and they offeered some to the guards, they refused it - at least when Popeye was looking. They kept going on pieces of black Kommmisbrot, with a rare slice of sausage. The only concession Popeye made was to allow us to share our precious cigarettes with them, and that meant more to them than all the rest.

One grey-haired guard was half-carrying a frail young Lieutenant. He had one arm round the American's waist, and with the other was holding his arm, which was draped over the German's shoulder. The young officer was taking short puffs at a cigarette and, since he was the only one with one arm free, he passed his cigarette to the guard to take a grateful draw, and then took it back to repeat the process until only a small butt was left. But no butts were ever thrown away. Both prisoners and guards would carefully pinch them out and stuff them in the pockets of the guards' grey greatcoats. Later they would be ground into the bowls of the small pipes most German soldiers carried, to be smoked at leisure.

Popeye and I conferred about our charges. We agreed that most of them seemed to be in bad shape. One had broken his leg while stumbling and falling in the ruts and the snow; one seemed to have pneumonia; and one had continued to walk on badly blistered feet until the entire leg was frozen and stiff.

I asked Popeye about doctors. There had been a few in camp, but they had been responsible for all Compounds, North, South and Centre. Presumably, they were either with other marchers, which we heard were suffering even more than us, or more likely the doctors had been commandeered to serve with the front-line combat troops.

As our sad little group stumbled and lumbered painfully across the wintry Silesian plains and our pace got ever slower, I realised we had to get medical help - or we, too, would become the Legion of the Damned.

"There's a hospital a few miles away," said Popeye. "Let's get the worst cases there."

When we reached the hospital and the wagons lurched to a stop we stared at an unbelievable sight. In front of the building was a wide-open, snow-covered slope and across it a long line of wounded German soldiers lay in the snow. There must have been more than three hundred of them. I turned to the German officers.

"Are they all waiting for treatment?"

They nodded. They'll never let us in, I thought. We'll never even get to the door.

Slowly and carefully, we unloaded our fragile charges and dragged them up the slope, past the line of German soldiers. Some of them were seriously wounded, lying on stretchers. Some seemed just as badly wounded, but were just lying in the snow. Most were crudely bandaged, but the bandages were soaked with blood, some of it old and black, some of it fresh and bright crimson. Others of them showed no sign of being wounded, except for their grey faces and red, staring eyes. All of them simply lay there motionless.

As we limped slowly past them, some looked at us with expressionless, staring eyes. Others didn't even turn to look. Those few hundred yards seemed endless as we hobbled up the snowy slope under the gaze of those ghostly, quiet, beaten soldiers. They were past fear, past despair, past pain, past caring.

When we finally reached the door, the German officer explained to the receiving orderly that we were American officers with wounded. He shrugged and disappeared. When he returned, to my surprise he led us past the waiting wounded German soldiers into a large hall. It was crowded.

Every inch of floor was covered with beds, stretchers and tables, nearly all being used as operating tables. Even the large staircase was covered with stretchers and mattresses. The whole place was a Dante's Inferno. Most of the operations seemed to be amputations, and I remembered that the Germans probably had little or no penicillin. Some of those doing the operations were women. I wondered if they were qualified surgeons, or nurses drafted in to try to help in the hopeless task.

The orderly pushed our boys into the front of the line waiting to be treated, and started to explain. The haggard young doctor shrugged, finished off the case he'd just been handling and started on one of our men. He had long ago given up trying to give priorities to those he treated. He was simply going through the motions until he dropped.

I turned away from this slaughter-house and escaped into the open air. The German officers and guards had waited outside, but they kept apart from the long line of wounded. I understood. Facing those staring eyes, you felt embarrassed at being in one piece.

One of the German officers asked another if he had a cigarette. He knew the answer, but he knew I was in earshot. I took a pack from my pocket and offered him one. He took it carefully, broke it in two and gave one half to his colleague. As they lit up, I saw the gaze of the wounded soldiers slowly turn to look at them. I went over and shook out a cigarette. I passed them out until there were none left. They took them reverently, but still in a daze. Sometimes, when they couldn't move their hands, I put the cigarette between their black, swollen, frost-bitten lips. One was a mere boy. His smooth, almost girlish face stood out amongst the unshaven faces of the others. He lay there unmoving, his pale blue eyes just staring. I put a cigarette between his lips, but the man lying next to him shook his head.

"Der ist tot," he said. He is dead.

We had to leave one PoW at the hospital. It was dark as Popeye and I plodded after the rest of the column. We finally caught up with the tail-end group. To my surprise, Jim Devinney was with them.

It was bitterly cold, but Jim was in light khaki slacks and a flight jacket. He'd been shot down over the Ploesti oilfields on the low-level raid which had taken off from Southern Italy and he still wore the summer flying gear he'd been shot down in. If he'd been issued with heavier clothes, he'd bartered them for more essential comforts like cigarettes and chocolate. Jim was in bad shape; he was obviously running a high fever and I thought he was coming down with pneumonia. He seemed to have trouble recognising me but when he did, he dug his hand in his flight jacket pocket and produced a small block of chocolate.

"Here," he said. "I've been looking for you. I figured you might need this."

"Thanks. I'll split it with you."

We started to march on, but it was clear we couldn't go much further. It was late and it had been a long, hard day. I told Popeye our little group of stragglers could never catch up with the main column, which was probably already in Muskau. We all needed rest and couldn't go any further.

There was a barn at the side of the road. There wasn't much hay in it, but we scraped together what we could and bedded down. Jim was lying beside me. From time to time, he broke into violent shivering and shaking. I moved over and took him in my arms to warm him up - and perhaps to get warmer myself. But it did no good.

I got up and stamped around, slapping my arms around my body. I walked to the back of the barn and looked outside. There was a manure pile in the yard. The farm animals had been taken away but the dung heap was steaming. I remembered that they generate heat. I went over and scooped out a hollow in the pile. There was a good mixture of straw in the manure, but as I burrowed into the mound, I felt the heat. I went back to Jim and shook him. Although he was still shaking, he didn't seem to know what was going on. I dragged him out to the manure, put him in the hollow I had made and cradled him in my arms as I lay beside him.

A stocky figure emerged from the shadows. It was Popeye. He handed me a clove of garlic which he had found hanging up under the eaves, and a chunk of black bread.

"This will give you strength."

"If it doesn't kill me!" I said, but I knew he was right.

I forced some into Devinney's mouth, and he seemed to eat it. Then I slowly chewed my garlic, eating the bread at the same time to cut down on the strong, stinging taste. On the march I had learned that garlic gave a lot of strength and I had gradually got used to the taste.

Popeye nodded towards Devinney. "Is he alright?"

"He's still shaking," I said. "I'm trying to keep him warm."

Popeye moved over and lay down beside us. "Gestatten Sie, Herr Major? - May I?" he asked.

In the morning, Jim was almost his old self.

"Next time you want to sleep with me, don't eat garlic. It was worse than the manure!" he said.

"Don't knock it - it probably saved your life!"

When we reached Muskau, the rest of the Compound was there, preparing their morning coffee. They had camped in a brickyard overnight, an ideal place for Kriegies. Two bricks with a Klim can on top and wood shavings underneath made the perfect stove for heating water.

I was told that somehow a train had been organised and we were due to start loading in two hours.

It was a freight train, but it looked good to us. As we expected, it was to take us to Bavaria, the part of Germany which was least menaced, and near the so-called "Redoute", where rumour had it the Nazi leaders would make a last-ditch stand, finally using senior officer PoWs as hostages.

"What's the name of our new camp?" I asked Popeye.

"Moosburg," he said. "It's a satellite camp. The main camp is called Dachau."

*****

Chapter 3

"WITHOUT ME"

The train trip from Silesia to Bavaria was no great hardship after the rigours of the march. There was room to stretch out in the box cars. The train often stopped in the countryside, and whilst the guards swung down from their posts at the front and rear of each freight car and covered us with their guns, the bolts were shot open and the doors slid back. We jumped down, stretched, joked and relieved ourselves.

There were many long stops, but we were in no hurry. When we were in a town or station, the doors were kept closed, but sometimes the delays were long, so they had to let us out. Then it was that we saw the bomb damage, the ruin of the stations and the cities, the ruin in the grey, expressionless faces, the ruin of the Thousand Year Reich, the Nazi dream.

Knowing the end was near made it easier for us to put up with captivity, being moved, being prisoners, because now there was hope, now we could see the end.

Eventually, the train arrived at Moosburg. It was a typical, pleasant Bavarian country town and on the march from the station to the camp, we saw the neat half-timbered buildings, many with walls painted with old colourful scenes and Gothic writing. There were even windowboxes, which in summer would be full of bright red geraniums.

Even the main gate of the prison camp was not unattractive. Over the top of it, forming an arch, was a painted wooden carving which depicted prisoners at work, with the motto "Arbeit Macht Frei" - Work makes one free.

And to a certain extent, that was true; at least it was true for the NCOs and privates, who went out to work. But for the officers there was no relief from the confinement of the camp. After the brief breath of freedom during the march, Moosburg seemed to be under a drab, grey, suffocating pall.

Sagan had been sparse and bare, but at least it was clean and new and airy. Moosburg was an old camp, probably originally built for enlisted

PoWs or perhaps, at one time, as barracks for German soldiers. It was more solidly built than Sagan, but the buildings were dark and there was little open space.

Worst of all was the crowding. It was already full when we arrived. In the inner officers' camp there were French, English, Serbian and others. Outside in the soldiers camp there were even more nationalities, including Indian, Russian and even Italians. But it was much easier for them. They went out on work parties almost daily to work on the farms and repair bomb damage on the railways or anywhere else. According to the Geneva Convention, officers could not be made to work, even if they wanted to, and the Germans adhered to this clause to the letter.

In Moosburg, we were re-united with Del Spivey and the other Senior Officers. He had greeted me with a salute, followed by a warm hug. He also showed me some sheets of paper on which he had laboriously pencilled what he called a Commendation. It was addressed to the Adjutant-General. I thanked him for what I thought was a generous but futile gesture - until, after the war, I received the same document, without a single change, from the Adjutant-General. It was typical of Del Spivey that he carried those crumpled sheets of paper with him through months of imprisonment, and all the excitement of liberation and repatriation, until he could present them personally in Washington. I still treasure it after all the many years.

The overcrowding in Moosburg got steadily worse. More prisoners kept arriving from east and west. One day the German Kommandant asked to see me. He had his counterpart from the outer camp with him.

"We have a problem with some Russian prisoners. You speak languages. Would you be good enough to help us?"

I have noticed that when you speak a few languages, people are inclined to think you speak all languages, just as they think that if you speak a few words of a language, you must speak it fluently.

"I only speak a few words of Russian," I said, "and anyway, you must have a Russian Vertrauensmann."

The Vertrauensmann, or "Man of Confidence", was the non-commissioned equivalent of Senior Officer.

The Kommandant obviously believed that one either spoke a language or didn't, with nothing in between.

"You speak Russian, and their Vertrauensmann is not co-operating. If we don't resolve this matter, there will be problems."

This was ominous. The Germans treated different nationalities with different degrees of respect. Highest on the list were the British, perhaps because they felt a certain sympathy with them, but mostly because the British demanded it. Then came the Americans, probably for similar, if less strong, feelings. The French probably came next, but then they had been beaten. Near the bottom of the list came the Russians. The Germans explained that Russia had not signed the Geneva Convention, but I felt it was more a reflection of the no-holds-barred fight to the finish on the Eastern Front.

In any case, I felt I'd better see if I could be of assistance to our allies, and try to avoid a German "solution" to the problem, which in the case of Russian prisoners-of-war might well be a few bursts of machinegun fire.

Von Braune and his escort led me through the barbed-wire gate of the officers' compound out into the labyrinth of the soldiers' compound and on to the reception area. On the way, the Kommandant explained that a newly-arrived group of Russian prisoners were flatly refusing to go through the regulation de-lousing procedure which every PoW underwent as a matter of course before entering a camp. It involved stripping and showering, while the clothing went through de-lousing treatment to be returned to its owner at the end of the process.

When we got to the scene of the "problem", I was astonished. German guards, menacingly pointing their guns, were surrounding a crowd of what looked to me like Chinese. It was as if a section of old Peking had been transported to Moosburg. They were of all ages and sexes, some dressed in quilted tunics and trousers, others in leather coats. There were children, young men and women, old men and women, middle-aged men and women. Some wore pigtails, some wore round hats, some had a kind of hood. All of them were small. All of them were Oriental.

The only Russian uniform I saw was that of the Russian man of confidence, who seemed completely disinterested in spite of a machinegun pointed at him. Von Braune introduced me to him, but he gave no indication that he understood a word.

"Comrade Sergeant," I said, "I'm an American officer, can I be of any help?"

At least in those days, half the secret of communicating with the Russians was liberal use of the word "Tovarisch" - comrade.

In this case, he sprang to life, saluted me smartly and then embraced me with enthusiasm. Maybe the salute was in response to the "Sergeant" and the bear hug handled the "Tovarisch".

"What's going on?" I asked.

"I've been trying to tell these idiots that these people are from Mongolia and don't understand Russian, and even if I could speak to them, they would never take off their clothes. They believe they could catch cold and die, and they probably would!"

"But who are these people? They can't be soldiers!"

"They're part of the People's Army," he said.

I had heard of hordes of Russians being driven forward from behind against German positions, of German machineguns mowing them down until the guns got so hot they jammed, and the mass of humanity engulfing the Germans, leaving the way open for the regular army to come through, but until now I had dismissed these tales like the other rumours that run wild in wartime. But looking at these strange little creatures from another world, I had to believe it was true.

In any case, I thought I had the solution to the Kommandant's problem.

"These are not military prisoners-of-war. They have no papers, no uniforms, no officers, no military status. They are civilians and you would be wrong to accept them in an already over-crowded camp."

It was typical of the German wartime mentality that it had never occurred to the Kommandant to question the administrative orders that had sent these poor people to his camp. They had arrived with the proper instructions, therefore they had to be taken in.

Now, however, both officers grasped the idea enthusiastically.

"That's right, these are not soldiers, they are civilians. Civilians are not our responsibility. We must insist on that!"

After this judgement of Solomon, I went back to the compound with Popeye. I had a twinge of conscience about the Mongols, especially the old and the young.

"What will happen to them now?" I asked.

He shrugged. "Maybe labour camps. Anyway, the war will soon be over and the Russians will take them back. Better in the labour camps!"

Things got even worse after the Battle of the Bulge. There were now big "purges" of Americans, but worse than the increased overcrowding was the blow to morale. We couldn't understand what had happened and, what was worse, when we talked to the new PoWs, they didn't seem to know what had happened either. We realised once again the big difference between aircrew and infantry.

We not only knew what was going on but, especially in the case of fighter pilots, we had planned it and then put it into action. We were to a certain extent independent free agents, holding our fate in our own hands. Talking to the infantry, I got the impression that for most of the war they were moved about like pawns on a chess-board, never really seeing the whole game, and this produced a kind of blank fatalism. "Theirs not to reason why..."

Now, for the first time for over a year, the lines on our maps showed German advances as von Rundstedt's tanks thrust towards Antwerp. It didn't last long. When the weather cleared and the Air Force could get into action again, the danger was over. But there was a feeling of frustration and depression, only slightly relieved by McAuliffe's stand at Bastogne, and his typically American reply to the German demand to surrender: "Nuts!"

I remember about this time making a morning inspection tour of the Compound. It was snowing and sleeting, so the Kriegies had to find shelter to brew up their morning coffee and toast their Kommisbrot. Almost the only place was the Aborts. These were not like the simple wooden latrines of Sagan, but solid old buildings with concrete floors. It was a constant battle to keep them clean, making sure the cess-pools underneath were regularly emptied to avoid the horrors of an overflow.

I pushed my way past those waiting to get into the latrine, but had to stop when I stepped inside. The place was dark and full of smoke. Every toilet seat was occupied, with others hovering around waiting their turn. Every inch of space on the floor was occupied by squatting men, intent on brewing their coffee in Klim cans. Picking my way through the gloom and smoke, through the men coughing and sniffing and wiping the tears from their stinging eyes, I stepped past two Kriegies bent over their Klim can stove, fanning and blowing to keep the little flame going, holding the slices of bread against the can and carefully placing each piece of toast on a brick placed next to the cans, so as to keep it out of the wet and slime on the floor. As I passed, I heard a remark, in a completely unemotional voice, which summed up the whole atmosphere, and the depths to which we had sunk.

"Your nose is dripping on the toast."

It wasn't any one thing in particular. It was the war, seemingly dragging on for ever. It was the worry of what would happen when the war did end. Would we be taken into the Redoute and used as hostages? Would the Russians join forces with the Germans against the capitalist West, leading to a war without end? It was the overcrowding. It was the constant shortage of food. It was the continuing deterioration in our living standards. It was the loss of freedom, the being a prisoner; and only those who have been in captivity can know how soul-destroying it can be.

Nerves were frayed on both sides. One day, a work party from the camp outside our officers' compound came in to repair the barbed wire fences. I never knew exactly what happened. There appeared to be some confusion, followed immediately by a burst of machinegun fire. When it was over, a body hung like a rag doll on the barbed wire fence.

It was still there the next day. I protested to the Kommandant. His reply was typical of the difference in the Nazi's attitude to different nationalities.

"Why are you concerned? It's only a Russian!"

"It's a question of common decency and respect for the dead!"

I knew this would get results. The Nazis were very sensitive about any reflection on their standards of correct behaviour. Apparently there had been problems getting a work party to recover the body, so the

Germans finally did it themselves. The incident was not typical, and to me showed how standards were slipping under the strain.

But the thing that triggered off the main trouble was not Nazi brutality; it was the latrines.

Whenever large numbers of people are forced to live together, the loudest complaints revolve around latrines and food; cans and canteens. As more and more prisoners were herded into the camp, and the melting snow and rain reduced everything to a mire, the facilities could not cope. Two or three times the Aborts had overflowed, but the "Honey-wagon" had arrived before the situation became serious.

Then came the day when, after hours of sleet, rain and snow, the cess-pool overflowed, flooding the Abort buildings and spreading out in rivulets into the compound. Popeye went off to find the honey-wagon. I raised hell with the Kommandant. We learned that, under the strain of constant action, the honey-wagon had broken down. Another had been ordered from a different compound, but no-one knew when, or if, it would arrive.

By the time Appel was called, the tension was electric. There was no question of standing still to be counted. The men rushed around and shouted. The Kommandant had turned up, in addition to the Lager Offizier. He ordered in all available guards and they were all armed. The Kommandant told me to order the PoWs to co-operate and, I refused.

"They have justifiable grievances. It is up to the German military command to treat officer prisoners in a civilised manner! When you are fulfilling your obligations, we will co-operate!"

Most of the guards brought in were not Luftwaffe men, but Wehrmacht infantry personnel. They had no experience of Air Force officers, and had certainly never heard any prisoner talk to any German officer, let alone a Colonel, as I had. Their immediate reaction was to cock their sub-machine guns and point them in my direction. When the Kriegies heard the rattle of the guns being cocked and saw them being brought up and aimed, they roared their disapproval, and started to surge forward.

The first guard to cock his gun had advanced close to me to make his threat more menacing. As the crowd started forward, I saw him swing his gun away from me towards the PoWs. It was the instinct of the fighter-pilot - attack! I grabbed his gun, twisted it and ripped it out of his hands. The other guards saw me with a gun in my hands. Every one of them aimed at me; but the quick reaction stayed with me. Out of the corner of my eye, I saw a grey uniform rushing at me. It was Popeye. I threw the gun to him. He caught it. I followed up.

"Herr Feldwebel! Get your men under control!"

Without hesitating, he lashed into the disarmed guard and dismissed him. Then he took control. He ordered the other guards to put up their guns. The PoWs had stopped in their tracks. Popeye marched up to the German Kommandant, saluted and said something I couldn't hear. But I didn't need to. The Kommandant came up to me and saluted. He was obviously looking for a way out. Quietly, he said to me: "What now?"

I knew we had won. "We are Air Force," I said. "Get the other guards out of here!"

He turned and barked an order to Simoleit, the Lager Offizier, who passed it on to Popeye. The green uniforms of the infantry guards disappeared.

Then the compound gates were flung open, and into the camp galloped the honey-wagon. Again I took the initiative. I saluted the Kommandant.

"Alles erledigt!" I told him. All is handled.

Without waiting, I swung round and shouted "Camp, dismiss!"

The Kriegies dispersed. The German officers saluted and left, happy to get away as soon as possible. The guards followed them. I saluted Del Spivey.

"We won!" I said.

"We sure did!" he said, saluting in return.

I was left alone. I couldn't believe it was over. I couldn't believe we'd got away with it. It was a miracle that no shots were fired, that no-one had been killed.

Out of the growing dusk, a grey figure approached. He saluted me;

not with the Nazi salute which had been imposed since the attempt on Hitler's life, but with the old military salute. I drew myself up and saluted back.

"Danke!" I said.

"Ich hab' zu danken! - I thank you!" said Popeye.

Soon after, Del Spivey and the other Colonels, with Bill Brown to act as their interpreter, were taken off to Berlin by Burger, the German Luftwaffe General responsible for PoW camps, in an attempt to make arrangements for talks to end the hostilities in Europe.

The mission was doomed to failure from the start. The Allies knew that it was only a matter of weeks before their armies would meet up, and the Nazis were determined to fight to the last and would quickly block any attempt by other, less fanatical Germans, to do otherwise.

This left Colonel Smith and myself responsible for what had been the Centre Compound of Stalag Luft III.

The Allies were closing in on all fronts. In fact, they seemed to be moving as far as they wanted to. Now when the senior officers discussed the situation, our concern was not when the war would be over, but what would happen to us when our captors saw that we were about to be liberated. There was open talk of the officers being taken into the Redoute, the mountain area south-east of the camp near Berchtesgaden, to be used as hostages. I had been discussing it, and mulling over the best course of action for us, and finally made a formal proposal to Colonel Smith.

"Up until now, you've made it clear that my duty was to stay with the camp and not to attempt to escape, because of the help I could give to the Kriegies, and I've agreed. But now I think the best thing I can do for all concerned is to get out of here and try to meet up with the U.S. army. I've got the necessary rank. My German is fluent and so is my French. Leclerc's Free French are with the Americans on this front and I might meet them. Hodges' army is headed straight for us. If I can get to them, they could do a pincer movement around the camp and block any attempt to move us into the mountains."

"How do you think you'll get out?" he wanted to know.

"I've done some homework. The next time a work party comes into our camp, I can switch with one of them and get out to the outside camp. Then when they send out a normal work party to work on the railroad, I'll be on it and find a way to escape."

He obviously didn't like the idea.

"But it's the best way to make sure they don't use us as hostages."

"That's not what I'm worried about," he said.

"What then?"

"I'm afraid you'll get yourself killed!"

The Germans had done everything possible to prevent any contact between the officers and the soldier PoWs in the outside camp. It was the same phobia that had such tragic results after the Great Escape: the fear of a mass uprising by the prisoners. But as the end of the war became inevitable and ever closer; as the crowding got worse and the overworked guards got more dispirited, I had been able to learn something of the outside camps. From getting close to the work parties that came into our compound to make repairs, take out garbage, and so on, I learned that they usually came from the Serbian camp.

It was easy to find out that the Vertrauensmann of the Serbs was named Markovics. It was a little harder to slip a note addressed to him to one of the work party while someone was offering the guards a cigarette. The timing had to be perfect. The two German guards were at opposite ends of the work party as it started to march out of our camp. Simultaneously, two German-speaking Kriegies started to stroll in the opposite direction so that they would pass the work party, each one being beside one of the guards at the same time. Meanwhile, I was poised to pass the centre of the column at the same moment, so that when the two Kriegies offered their cigarettes to each guard, I would pass my note to the nearest Yugoslav worker.

Our timing was okay, but when our boys offered their cigarettes, the guards curtly waved them away and continued to march, keeping their eyes steadily on their work party and on me. I had no alternative but to keep going. I looked straight at the guard who was bringing up the rear of the party. As we passed, he saluted. He recognised either me, or the rusty oak-leaves of the insignia on the shoulders of my shabby flight jacket. In any case, it gave me the opportunity I needed.

"Do you want the officers kept away from your column?"

"Jawohl, Herr Major, those are our orders."

Because of the crowding, the working party column was having some trouble marching through. I immediately went up the column waving the officer PoWs aside, until I was about mid-way between the guard at the front and the guard bringing up the rear. Without turning my head, I addressed the nearest Yugoslav in German.

"I have a note for your Vertrauensmann, Marcovics. I will give it to you when the guards are not watching. Do you understand?"

I waited for a reply that didn't come. Finally, I had to risk turning to look at the man. The urgent appeal in my eyes must have conveyed something to him. He replied in the universal Kriegie-deutsch we used throughout the camp, "Nix verstehen". The man didn't understand German.

Waving my arms and yelling to clear the path, I moved up to the next man ahead. Urgently I asked him, "Verstehen Sie Deutsch?" We were getting close to the guarded exit gate where the Yugoslavs would be counted and passed through. I had to have an answer, and it came. "Jawohl!"

I hurriedly repeated my message just as we reached the gates. The rear guard was coming up as the work party halted. He saluted me and thanked me and turned to help his colleague count their charges on their way through the gate.

There were four guards on the gate, plus the two with the work party, but they were all in front of me. I turned inwards towards the German-speaking Yugoslav and stepped right in front of him with my back to the gate and the guards. At the same moment, I took my precious message from my flight jacket pocket and shoved it down the front of the coat of the surprised Yugoslav. I moved quickly away and then turned back to see if it had worked. He had his hand inside his coat. Slowly, he drew it out. There was no sign of a letter, so I guessed he had put it in an inside pocket.

The letter to Marcovics explained our reasons for my escape, and asked if he could arrange a switch with one of his men on a work party. We sat back and waited for a reply. None came. Each time a work party came into our compound, I hovered around waiting for a message, but there was nothing.

Then one day, a working party came in to try to clean up some of the gooey mess on the floor of one of the gloomy Aborts. The two German guards were at the two doors, avoiding the stench of the interior. When one guard moved away from the door, I slipped into the Abort. Before my eyes got accustomed to the darkness, someone had taken my officers' peaked cap and replaced it with the strange Serbian forage cap, with high peaks fore and aft, but flat in the middle. At the same time, I was bundled into a voluminous grey greatcoat. I was already wearing wooden clogs, as did most of the prisoners in Moosburg because of the constant mud, so there was no need to change. Someone wrapped a scarf round my chin. I saw someone slip out of the door wearing my cap. I was now part of the working party, joining in with the others, brushing out the slush.

When we had finished, the German guards called us out, formed us up in two lines and marched us out to the gate. Fortunately, there was a slight drizzle, and it was cold for April, so the greatcoat and scarf looked normal enough. I was more afraid of the reaction of the Kriegies, and particularly my friends. But if they recognised me - and some of them must have - they gave no sign.

The gate worried me. There was a collection of guards and ferrets, all of whom knew me. I hunched over and tried to shrink into the greatcoat. I must have overdone it. Just as I was passing through the gate, the guard made as if to stop me.

"What's wrong with you?"

Quickly, I let go an enormous sneeze, followed by loud, wet sniffs.

"Grippe!" I said, and he quickly stepped back and let me pass.

In the enlisted soldiers camp, I came into a different world. It was as if I had, with one step, leaped from America to the Balkans. In our compound, I had been surrounded by the familiar sound of American voices; here it seemed that they spoke everything except English. If at one time the Germans had kept the different nationalities apart, now they were all mixed together in a wild Tower of Babel. The dominant atmosphere seemed to be that of the East. There were Slavs, Serbs, Croats, Russians, Poles, French, Italians. There were turbaned Moslems from Yugoslavia and the French African colonies. There were bearded, turbaned Sikhs from the British Indian regiments. There were Mongols,

Zoaves, Senegalese, Spahis, Ghurkas; every race under the sun.

The barrack blocks were basically the same as the ones I had just left in our officers' compound. Our barracks were stark and naked and few of us had any personal belongings. By contrast, these looked homier and more lived in. These men had been here a long time, and because they went out to work, they could barter and bargain in the outside world.

In fact, there was a kind of bazaar in the camp where almost anything could be had for a price. The principal currency was American cigarettes, but anything could be traded. Non-smokers became wealthy, particularly if they belonged to the chosen few who had access to Red Cross parcels. The Sikhs were very popular, not only because they were smiling, friendly and dignified but, much more important, as members of the British Armed Forces, they got Red Cross parcels, and because of their religion, they ate no meat and most of them didn't smoke cigarettes.

Many of the prisoners had been captured in North Africa and put into prison camps in Italy. When the Germans were forced out of Italy, they moved the prisoners to Germany. So mixed in with Eastern Europeans, Western Europeans, Asians and Africans, there were Australians, New Zealanders, South Africans and Rhodesians, most of whom had been captured at Tobruk. The Yugoslavs proudly ushered me through this jolly, jostling throng to their barracks.

I never quite understood why the Germans treated the Yugoslav partisans like regular PoWs, but condemned other irregular troops like the French to death. I was told that it was because France had officially surrendered and Yugoslavia had not. In my opinion, it was just another instance of the different ways the Germans rated various nationalities and handled them accordingly.

In any case, the Yugoslavs seemed to enjoy the same privileges as anyone else and had even more freedom. I was taken through a crowded barracks into a small cubicle at the end. Here, six men were sitting around a rough table between the bunks which lined the walls. It was just like the Blockleiter's room in our barracks.

There was no doubt about who was the leader. Marcovics was short and stocky, and he exuded an air of confidence and authority. He had fought with Tito and was obviously treated with the respect due to a national hero, He waved me to a seat at the wooden table.

Little did we know as we sat opposite each other, looking into each other's eyes, that some twenty years later we would be in the same position in Marcovics' vast office in Belgrade, where he was Minister of Industry and we were negotiating an international contract!

I explained our concern about being used as hostages, and he enthusiastically agreed that there should be contact with the rapidly advancing Allied armies. He spoke good German.

"Good! You go out on the next suitable work party. We will provide what you need, pistol with about 50 rounds of ammunition; a detailed map of the area, large-scale; compass and so on. We will get everything! In the meantime, of course, you cannot stay with us."

"Why not?"

"Already at this evening's Appel they will know you've gone. Ours was the only work party in the camp today. They will be here looking for you right after Appel. You must go at once!"

"Where?"

"I think to the South Africans."

I thought that I had misunderstood him. Surely he meant "Amerikaner" rather than "Sud Afrikaner".

"No! They are big, like you, and the Germans will not search so thoroughly there!"

The South African barrack blocks were spotlessly clean and the men themselves were well turned out in summer khaki uniforms. Marcovics turned me over to the South African Vertrauensmann, clapped me on the shoulder, and left. The South African sergeant stuck out his hand.

"Van den Hoevel," he said.

Once again, I explained why I was there.

"I'm sorry the Yugoslavs have saddled you with me, but they seemed to think I'd be better off with you."

"It's a pleasure! They may be right. The goons don't bother us so much."

"Why's that?"

"I suppose they think of the Boer War, and us being more Afrikaans than British. Maybe they even think some of us have their ideas. When we first got here, they expected us to join them. They asked us to join their army!"

"How many did?"

"None! But they still treat us with more respect, and that suits us fine!"

There was another advantage. The other PoWs also seemed to leave the South Africans alone. They had been taken prisoner at Tobruk, along with the Australians and New Zealanders, and there seemed to be some bad feeling on both sides. Then too, to my surprise, most of them were Afrikaners and Afrikaans was their native tongue.

Van den Hoevel took me to his barrack block.

"This is an American officer who'll stay with us overnight. Take care of him and give him khakis and a uniform cap. The Jerries'll be here looking for him in a minute. They're already combing the rest of the Lager."

He was right. I'd got into a voluminous pair of "shorts", which came to below my knees, puttees and boots, a khaki shirt and a round khaki cap and I'd shaved my black moustache. Then they were there. There were German soldiers and officers I'd never seen, mostly in the green uniform of the army, but there was Feldwebel Schulze from the Abwehr and other guards from our camp and, bringing up the rear, Major Simoleit, our Lager Offizier.

They went through block after block. The one I was in was the most crowded. Van den Hoevel called his men to attention as the Germans came through the barracks. I was surrounded by other men and, since they had been through the whole vast camp, the Germans didn't seem to be scrutinising us too keenly. I was worried when Schultze came by, but the big danger was Simoleit. After all, we'd seen each other almost daily for nearly a year, chatting in German and sometimes even in French while the Appel was going on. He was proud of his French. It proved his point that the Austrians were more civilised than the

Germans!

Sure enough, when he came opposite our group he stopped. I dared not look at him. After what seemed like an age, he moved on. But as I let out my breath, he turned and sauntered back. He seemed to be interested in a photograph pinned to one of the lockers. Finally, he turned away. The other Germans were half-way down the block. As Simoleit passed me, I heard him murmur in his clipped, German-accented French:

"Très chic, le chapeau!"

The next evening, Marcovics was back.

"We can get you out on a work party tomorrow morning."

I changed back into my old clothes and followed him back to his block. There we held a meeting in Marcovic's room. I was to go out on a work party to repair railway lines, an almost constant labour as the Tactical Air Force disrupted the communications in front of the advancing army.

"You'll need these."

Marcovics produced a map of the area, identification papers, a compass, a vicious-looking knife and finally a German Luger pistol, with ammunition.

"We have a contact for you in town, but don't write it down: Peter Gegner, Muhlheimerstrasse 26."

Dinner was served. The Yugoslavs ate better than we had in the American officers' camp. Meat was scarce, but the precious morsels were cooked into a delicious stew with potatoes, onions, kohlrabi and garlic. Vegetables were relatively plentiful thanks to the working parties who went out to work on the farms. They even had ersatz coffee, which made up for taste with strength.

Somehow they found a bunk for me. The Yugoslavs never seemed to be at a loss for anything.

As usual, there was bombing during the night, so the working party was sure to have plenty of work to do. Repairing the rail lines was now a constant task for PoWs throughout Germany and it was a losing battle for the Germans. Germany had become like Normandy after D-Day, when we kept anything from moving on the railways or even on the roads, except at night.

At five a.m. someone woke me up. After more ersatz coffee, the work party formed up. Neither the two guards on the party nor the guards on the gate seemed to take much interest in us. They were war-weary, depressed and discouraged, and anyway, who would want to risk escape now with the end of the war in sight?

We marched out into the roads and countryside of Bavaria. It was spring, and the bright sunshine, the green fields, the neat white churches with their onion-shaped spires, the farm houses with their deep over-hanging roofs, the cows in the fields, the horse-drawn carts, the friendly people, mostly women in their long old-fashioned skirts and bodices, all made a joyous contrast to the dull, grey, sterile world of the prison camp we'd left behind. Best of all was the smell. It was the smell of cows, the smell of hay, the smell of freshness, the smell of freedom.

As we passed the farm wagons, sometimes pulled by oxen or even cows, I looked at the women driving them. They wore kerchiefs on their heads, dresses and sometimes aprons and, on their feet, men's-style boots. Once more, I had the feeling I so often had in Germany, of being in another, older age.

The road we were on was well-paved and well-signposted. At the beginning of each village, a neat metal sign gave its name, followed by the name of the Kreis. Other signs indicated the direction and distances of neighbouring villages and, in larger letters, the next towns, exactly as I had seen them in the north when I was shot down.

After only an hour's march, we came to a railway crossing and turned onto the tracks. The prisoners marched in single file on either side of the tracks, with a guard at the front and one at the rear.

Gradually, the railway embankment got higher and we came to a bridge across a river. The bridge was undamaged, but on the embankment on either side were small bomb craters around which the broken railway tracks twisted like writhing snakes. I thought back to the days when we had dive-bombed bridges, almost always unsuccessfully. A railway bridge is a small target, and even when a bomb hits it, it can glance off or even explode without doing much damage. On this bridge, the planes of the Tactical Air Force had obviously lined up on the railway lines to make sure they had at least a reasonable chance of hitting the tracks somewhere along their length.

By now, the procedure for repairing the damage was routine and simple. The guards indicated where the damaged rails should be unbolted from the wooden ties, the bomb craters were filled in, ties and tracks were taken from reserve stocks already placed at the side of the tracks and relaid to replace the damaged ones.

It went very fast, and by noon the track had been replaced on one side of the bridge.

The head guard, who wore the stripes of an Obergefreiter or corporal, ammounced that we would cross the bridge and have a lunch break before tackling the work on the other side.

The bridge was a steel structure which carried only the two railway tracks. Between the ties were gaps through which one could look down to the river below. It wasn't easy to cross on foot. You had to watch every step. I noticed that even the guards kept their eyes down as they carefully stepped from one tie to the next.

It had been agreed that the best time for me to slip away from the work party was when the work was over at dusk. I turned to Stefan, a sergeant and the leader of the Yugoslav work party.

"Do we have to come back over the bridge to get back to camp?"

He nodded.

"Ohne mich - without me!" I said.

He nodded again.

The afternoon's work was a repitition of the morning routine. There was less repair work, so the working party slowed down. The guards didn't mind. As long as the work got done and they could report the lines safe again, they were quite happy to sit in the sun rather than return to the gloomy camp. So it was getting dark when the last repair was made and we shouldered our tools and began to cross the bridge.

The head guard led the way and the other one brought up the rear. I hung back and started over the bridge at the same time as the guard. When I saw that he was carefully picking his way across without raising his eyes, I slowed down until the rest of the party was well ahead of me. Stefan and the others also slowed down when they saw me dropping back, so that the guard was only aware that some prisoners were around him, without noticing anyone in particular.

When they were far enough ahead of me in the gloom, I turned and started back. I listened for them to get to the other side. It was then that the guard might check and discover me missing. But I kept moving. As soon as I got back to the end of the bridge, I turned and slithered down the embankment. Then I ducked into the bushes and weeds along the bank and waited.

As I rolled over and lay on my back looking up at the darkening sky, I had a strange feeling.

I'd slept in lots of strange places; the bunks at Sagan, the manure pile on the march, the crowded barracks in Moosburg; but this was somehow different. And then I knew. For the first time in almost a year, I was free. Not for long, maybe. And not out of danger, but still, at least for the time being, I was free. It was if a heavy load had rolled off me. I stretched out and arched my back. It was as if, for all the months as a prisoner I had always walked with a stoop and never straightened up. Maybe all prisoners are permanently stooped.

*****

Chapter 4

"LIFE IS FUNNY - AND SAD"

Soon it was almost dark, and still no hue and cry. I got up and started off down the river bank in the direction of Moosburg. Far away to the east, there were rumblings and dull flashes, either bombs or artillery. But what excited and thrilled me was the strong smell of spring; the damp of the river, of the green fields, the cows, the farmyards, the fresh earth. It was the promise of an end to greyness, to prison camp, to war and death, and the beginning of life.

When I arrived at the town, I climbed up the bank beside a bridge. I found myself on a street flanked by typical Bavarian houses. Moosburg was too small to have been bombed. There was no sign of war. The lighted windows were homely and friendly in the neat, quaint houses with carved eaves and painted walls and geranium window-boxes in the style of Hansel and Gretel. It was that German contrast again. How could people who lived in such houses make total war? Was it possible that the prison blocks were only a mile away, and the main concentration camp of Dachau only a few miles beyond?

There was a curfew, so the dark streets were deserted except for a few uniformed police, small bands of soldiers and smartly-marching Hitler Jugend, boys of 12 to 15 pledged to defend the Fatherland to the death. I knew my PoW khaki was dangerous, so I stepped into the dark gardens and hid in the shadows of the hedges and walls when anyone approached.

I had to get to the town centre to get my bearings so that I could follow directions to the address I had.

When I got there, I found a large house divided into flats. I pressed the button for first floor, No. 26, and waited. The front door was opened by a young man in the green uniform of the German army. Without speaking, he led me upstairs and into a small apartment.

"I'm Peter Gegner," he said in English. "This is my wife, Helga, and this is Dr. Schmidt, a leading member of our organisation."

Dr. Schmidt was balding and heavy-set and I wasn't surprised when he said, "I'm a professor."

He looked the part. Helga was slim and dark. All of them looked nervous.

"Shouldn't we speak German?" I asked.

"Of course," said Peter. "We didn't know you spoke it so well."

"Do you know anything else about me?"

"Of course - everything! But you know nothing about us. We are members of the South German Freedom Movement, which is part of the Anti-Nazi Underground Organisation."

"I'm amazed! I had no idea there was any anti-Nazi organisation in Germany! How long has this been going on?"

"Ah! You think we only start up now when the war is ending! No, we have existed all through the war. Even before, as Social Democrats. The movement was almost annihilated by the Nazis. Hundreds of thousands died in jails and concentration camps, but the flame was never quite extinguished. We went underground, we did what we could, we helped Nazi victims escape from Germany, we have recorded Nazi crimes, but above all, we have bided our time and prayed for our time for action to come. That time is now, and on the 25th we are going to have our day of action!

"We will lead a revolt and free Bavaria! Bavaria will not be conquered. We will welcome the Allies as our allies!"

"Don't you think the Allies are going to take over Bavaria anyway? You and your friends may be risking your lives for nothing."

Peter was very intense. "The world must see that there has been and is resistance to Nazism, otherwise they will condemn all Germans. We must show them there is a democratic movement here on which to build a new Germany."

I was sceptical, but this little group was so sincere, I wasn't going to argue with them. The main thing was that I thought I could trust them to help me. I needed to be hidden while the search was on, I needed other clothes. If I was to get to the advancing American forces I could only move during the daytime, because of the night curfew, and the

PoW khaki would give me away. Above all, I had to know where the U.S. Army was and how and where I could meet it.

It was agreed that I could hole up in their flat for the next day and night. Then I would set out for the nearest Allied advance troops, General Hodge's army. Peter had local maps showing where they thought the Americans would be and their probable line of advance.

"I think you can just get into one of my uniforms," he said.

"No way!" I said. "There's too good a chance of my being caught, and a PoW impersonating a German soldier, wearing a German uniform, would mean certain death. I'd rather risk being in civilian clothes."

Peter agreed reluctantly, and produced one of his pre-war suits. After Helga had lengthened the trousers and sleeves and pressed it, it was still a little small, but the meagre rations of the last few weeks had made me slim enough to get by.

They made up a bed for me on the floor of a small room not much bigger than a cupboard, and locked me in for the night.

Peter was recovering from wounds received on the Russian front. I had noticed a slight limp, but apparently he had had more serious machine-gun wounds in his stomach. In any case, he had not had any communication from his unit for a week, and had decided not to make any contact with the military, in order to be on hand for their big "Liberation" exercise in the Munich area. I thought their Freedom Movement was a little pathetic, but I admired their determination and enthusiasm. They were risking much more than I was, and I was grateful.

The next day proved the point. It was about 8 a.m. and I had just finished in the bathroom and returned to my cupboard when I heard a knock on the outside apartment door, and a quick warning knock on my own door, followed almost immediately by loud male voices in the flat. Doors were opened and closed. Then I heard heavy footsteps approaching my room.

Now I could hear the conversation. Peter was explaining why he was at home. I heard him reel off the names of Russian towns where he had fought. Then the footsteps arrived at my door - and stopped.

"And here?"

"A cupboard," said Peter.

They tried to open it, but I had locked it.

"Open it please." The voice was polite but firm.

Peter called out, "Helga, do we have a key to the Schmidt's cupboard?"

Then to the police, "The people from whom we rent the apartment have left a few of their own things in there."

There was a pause, during which I felt sure they would hear my heartbeat or breathing.

Then "Gut!" and the footsteps moved on.

When they had left, Peter came back and unlocked the door.

"How did we get away with that?" I asked.

"I think it was the uniform, the Iron Cross, and the Russian front. He'd been there, too. He could never believe a good German soldier could be untrue to the Fatherland."

I was relieved when they woke me early on the final morning. As soon as it was light, I solemnly shook hands with the brave threesome and tried to thank them. Helga had put half a loaf of bread and some precious sausage in a scarf carefully knotted, but I refused it, partly because I thought it would look suspicious, partly because I thought they would need it more than I, but mostly because I was too nervous to think about food.

Peter let me out of the front door and once more I was on my own. The town was well awake and, although there were lots of uniforms around, I was relieved to see a lot of civilians. I followed Peter's instructions to find the road we had chosen and soon I was out of town, striding out towards the west.

It wasn't a main road, but there was a fair amount of traffic. Coming from the west were the inevitable refugees, peasants walking alongside their horse-drawn wagons piled high with their belongings and children.

I wondered if they realised they were now suffering the fate of the millions of refugees who had fled before the German army since the war began. Probably not. Understanding the plight of others was not a characteristic of Nazi Germany.

Around me, moving west, were groups of soldiers. Most were in SS uniforms, moving quietly and confidently. Some were Hitler Jugend, bright-eyed and excited, marching in step, often singing army songs. Each group seemed isolated, loyal only to itself. There seemed to be no co-ordinated command.

About mid-morning came the sound of planes. When the noise got louder, I saw them; about ten low-flying P-47 Thunderbolts. They saw the road and turned to dive down. Everyone dived for the side of the road and flattened themselves against the ground. The road at that point was passing through wheat fields. I'd done enough strafing to know that the roadside wasn't safe, so I scrambled into the short, young wheat. It wasn't high enough to cover me, but at least I was away from the road.

It was the first time I'd been on the receiving end of strafing. The deafening noise of the machine-gun fire and roaring engines shook me. I saw at first-hand the destruction those eight machine guns could cause as men, wagons, animals and even the road itself were chewed up as one plane after another spat out its fire. This was what had stopped the German troops and Panzers from rushing to the Normandy beaches and throwing the invasion back into the sea. This was what had paved the way for the Allied advance across France and the Low Countries. This was what had prevented any movement on the roads by day, leaving a trail of knocked-out vehicles at the side of every road in Western Europe, and killed and wounded soldiers from privates to generals.

As I lay with my face in the mud of that field, I prayed that after surviving throughout the war I wouldn't be killed by friends in the familiar old "Thunderjug". And I understood the helpless frustration the German armies were feeling, knowing there was no defence, no retaliation, no protection against the overwhelming air superiority of the Allies.

When the planes had passed on, there was silence. Slowly, people got up and took care of the dead and wounded, or continued on their way. There was an unreal, dream-like quality about it. I looked out over the fields. The sun was still shining, the quiet cows were still peacefully grazing in the fields. There was peace in the midst of war.

All day I tramped on, but as dusk fell I worried and wondered about the curfew and the dark. Everyone else seemed to have somewhere to go, even if it was only to camp by the roadside. But in spite of catastrophe on the Eastern Front and the Western Front, in spite of the daily and nightly air-raids (Galland called Germany "Festung ohne Dach" - the fortress without a roof) - in spite of everything, the police, both military and civilian, were checking papers and making spot checks. The only papers I had were those which Peter had given me. I had little faith in them - and the pistol stuck in my belt might easily be spotted.

I had thought I might hole up in the wheatfields at the side of the road, but it was spring and the grain was short. Wherever I looked, there was no cover.

When it was getting dark, I turned off onto a cart track leading into the fields. It ended at a small cottage, with a few farm sheds behind.

I slunk into the farmyard, moved along the side of a small barn and pushed the door open. There was a small pile of hay against the back wall. I pulled the door closed behind me, went to the hay and tried to burrow into it. There wasn't any depth to it and I couldn't cover myself completely.

It couldn't have been more than twenty minutes before I heard the mooing of cows and a voice urging them on. They came squelching into the yard outside. I thought the door of the barn was sure to be opened. I could hear the movement of the cows getting nearer until I even heard their heavy breathing; but they lumbered past. The wooden door of the adjoining cow-shed opened and I heard the cows moving in under the constant urging of the farmer's voice. It was a young, soft voice. Suddenly, there was flickering light showing through the thin lines between the slats separating the barn I was in from the cow-shed. I got up from the hay and put my eye to a knot-hole, but almost immediately the light faded out. I thought the farmer must have put the cows in and had now left them for the night.

I turned away from the wall and almost at once the door of the barn swung open. I was blinking in the light of a lantern shining straight at me. I couldn't see what was behind the light. Almost as an automatic reflex, I whipped out the Luger from my belt and pointed it at the lantern.

"Licht aus!" I ordered. "Light out!"

At the same time, I moved quickly towards the light. As I did so, the flame was blown out. I reached for the farmer, caught his shoulder and stuck the pistol hard in his ribs. He was small, and I guessed he was just a boy. He didn't say a word; neither did I.

Now I had a problem. We couldn't stay as we were with me holding him at gun-point; I couldn't let him go, as he would immediately call for help. I had noticed that the house was small, but there would almost certainly be someone else there, especially if this was only a boy. Of course, the able-bodied men would be away in the army in any case but, even if there were only women and old men or youngsters, how could I keep control over all of them, even with my pistol?

"Sind sie allein hier?" "Are you alone here?"

No answer. In any case, I figured I had no choice.

"Heraus!" I said, digging the Luger deeper into his side and pushing him towards the door. I stumbled over some milk pails. I should have noticed them when I came in and realised he might come for them when it was time for the evening milking.

It was almost dark outside now. There was no chink of light from the tiny farmhouse, but that might just mean they were well blacked-out. We crossed the muddy farmyard and reached the farmhouse door. The boy hesitated and I gave him a push. From the pocket of his coat, which was too big for him, he fished a ring of large keys, unlocked the door and pushed it open. To my relief, all was dark inside.

I pushed the door closed behind us.

"Machen Sie Licht!" I ordered.

A match was struck. In front of me was a small figure in a large coat bent over an old oil lamp, the glass in one hand, the match in the other. On his head was an old hat. He carefully placed the glass on the lighted lamp, blew out the match and turned towards me. Yes, I thought, it's just a young boy - but then I pulled off the hat.

The face of a young woman was gazing at me. The grey eyes were wide open, but not in fright. There was a calmness and dignity there that made me feel a little ashamed.

I put the gun back in my belt, handed her hat back and said, "I'm sorry."

She just stood there with the hat in her hand.

"Bitte," I said, inviting her to relax. I took the hat and helped her out of her man's coat. Looking around, I saw a peg on the back of the door and hung them up.

The room was very small and obviously served as kitchen, dining room and sitting-room. There was a large old-fashioned Bavarian stove of the kind called Kakkelofen, encased in beautiful ceramic tile and serving as cooking range as well as for heating. Beside it was an armchair. In the middle of the room was a bare, round wooden table with two wooden chairs. There was a wooden sideboard with a few plates on it and that was all.

She was still standing there gazing at me with those blue-grey eyes.

"Bitte", I said again, indicating a chair. She sat down and I sat opposite. For perhaps a minute neither of us spoke. Her lack of reaction puzzled me. Was it just peasant dullness? No, not with her. Was it an attitude of fatalism as a result of the war and its approaching end? Or was she frightened but able to conceal it? I felt I had to get through to her, not because my life might depend on it, but because somehow it became important for me to break the barrier of her silence.

So I answered the questions she hadn't asked.

"I'm an American Air Force officer. I've escaped from the prison camp at Moosburg. I have to get to the American army so that I can lead them to liberate my friends in the camps before the Nazis kill them!"

She kept on looking at me, and I couldn't fathom her expression. I didn't know if she believed me, or even cared. I babbled on about the war being over, and how good that was, because now all the suffering and death would stop.

Finally, I ran out of conversation. It was like talking to myself, except that she never took her grey eyes off mine. I looked around the room. On the sideboard was a photograph of a young German soldier.

"Your father?"

Without turning her face, she said, "My husband."

It was the first time I had heard her speak. It was soft and low, and the strong Bavarian accent for some reason came as a surprise.

"On the front?"

"Yes."

"Where?"

"Yugoslavia."

I knew there wasn't much front left in Yugoslavia. The country was mostly controlled by the partisans, and the Russian army was moving fast across the Balkans towards Belgrade.

"Do you hear from him?"

"Not for four months."

"The postal system has probably broken down."

More silence.

I brought out my precious cigarettes and offered them. She shook her head.

"Are you hungry?"

Her question surprised me. It was the first time she had spoken except in answer to a question.

"Yes, but please don't go to any trouble."

She got up, and soon there was a tablecloth, two plates and a loaf of home-made bread on the table. She produced half a sausage and two knives.

"I have no coffee or tea, and no milk."

Of course, the cows hadn't been milked because I had interrupted.

"Oh, I'm sorry! The cows should be milked - come, I'll help you."

We each took a metal pail from the barn I had been in and went into the cow-shed. There were only two cows. We squatted by our cows and the old familiar sound of milk squirting into the pail took me back to my uncle's farm three thousand miles, ten years and what seemed like a lifetime away. As I milked away, I thought of that young boy that was me, longing for adventure as he milked those far-away cows, and even his wild imagination couldn't have dreamed up the adventures he would have had by the time he milked his next cow.

We brought the sweet, warm milk back to the house. Most of it went into a large pan in the pantry to be skimmed for cream and butter, but we took two warm mugfuls for ourselves, and sat down to our bread and sausage. I raised my mug and smiled.

"Prosit!" I said.

For the first time, she smiled.

"Prosit!" she replied.

I drank and then raised my mug to the photograph. "Here's to you and a quick return."

We both solemnly drank our milk.

"What's his name?"

"Kurt."

"To Kurt!"

"To Kurt!"

After we had finished our bread and sausage, she produced some cheese, which we ate with the rest of the bread. We didn't talk much, but finally, the question both of us must have been thinking about had to be asked.

"You know there's a curfew at night?"

She nodded.

"I can't go out."

Silence.

"May I spend the night here?"

"You have the gun!"

I laughed, pulled the Luger out of my belt and slid it across the table to her.

"It's not loaded then?"

"Try it!"

She picked it up and slipped off the safety catch. She pointed it at me. There was a flash from the gunbarrel and a resounding explosion. The bullet whistled past my head and thudded into the wall behind me.

I was so shocked, I never moved.

"My God! You're a cool one!" she said.

"So are you. But you missed!"

"No, I know how to shoot. But I really thought it was unloaded."

We both started to laugh.

But the world outside came crashing back in on us. There was a loud banging on the door. Almost immediately, it was flung open and I saw green uniforms and the German coal-scuttle helmet. Hanging on the chest of the soldier was the metal plate of the "Field Polizei". The other wore the helmet of the civilian police. Both carried machine-pistols. The third of the group was a Lieutenant of the military police. He wore his normal officers' cap and carried no gun except for the holstered pistol on his belt.

"Polizei! Polizei!" he said. "Papiere!"

It was always the damned papers they wanted.

The girl had gone to the sideboard and was producing a sheaf of papers from a drawer.

"We are farmers. This is our farm," she said.

He looked at me. "What are you doing here?"

I remembered Peter's reason for being at home. "Convalesent leave. Severely wounded on the East Front."

He looked at the gun on the table. "What's that for?"

She answered before I could. "They say the enemy is coming. We are ready for them!"

By now, the officer was going through her papers. He handed them back.

"And yours?" he said to me.

I awkwardly pushed back my chair and attempted to get up with one leg stretched out stiffly. "I'll get them."

"Forget it!" he said.

I sank back in relief. But it wasn't over yet.

"Who's that?"

He was looking at the picture of her husband on the sideboard.

"My brother, on the front in Yugoslavia," she said.

"What's through there?" He pointed to the other door.

"Our bedroom," she said.

"Search the house!" he ordered the two men.

"What are you looking for?" she asked.

"Spies, saboteurs, deserters, escaped prisoners-of-war. A high-ranking American officer has escaped from Moosburg."

"When you leave, you might look in the barn, under the hay," she said.

"Jawohl! Let's go!" he shouted to his henchmen.

To us, he said "Good luck!"

"Heil Hitler!" I replied.

Quickly, he gave the Nazi salute, shouted "Heil Hitler!"" and followed his men out of the door in an operatic exit.

I couldn't help applauding. "A great performance!" I said.

We sat back and finally breathed easily. We drank another mug of warm milk. We talked. We talked as if we had been together for years. Finally she began to yawn.

"When do you have to get up tomorrow?" she asked.

"Before dawn, to be ready to go as soon as it's light."

"Me too." And then, "Where will you sleep?"

"Here," I said, pointing to the floor, and started moving the chairs and table to make room. She nodded and went into the tiny bedroom. She soon came out with two of the large duvets the Germans prefer to sheets and blankets. They were simply sheets sewn together and filled with feathers. With one underneath and one on top, I would have a comfortable bed.

I walked to the bedroom door and looked in. There was the bed with its mattress, but no duvet. I smiled, went back and picked one of them off the floor, took it into the bedroom and threw it on the bed. She shrugged, went into the bedroom and came out with a china washbowl and jug. She put them both on the table, took a large kettle from the stove and filled both with steaming water.

"For you!" she said, leaving the bowl and taking the jug into the bedroom and closing the door. Beside the bowl, she had left a neatly folded clean washcloth and a very small piece of soap.

I undressed and carefully hung my suit over the back of a chair. It was already wrinkled and, although at that time no-one was too worried about wrinkled clothes, I didn't want too look too dishevelled. After a wash, I wrapped myself in the soft duvet and was soon asleep.

But not for long. I was first awakened by artillery fire, but it was not so near. Then came the drone of aircraft engines. This was followed by the shattering explosion of the first bombs and more staccato cracks of the anti-aircraft guns.

At first, I thought it would be Landshut, a few miles north of Moosburg. It was a rail centre and had an airfield; but then I realised they were hitting closer to us. The fact that they were bombing so close to Moosburg meant they didn't know the location of the PoW camps.

It went on for about half an hour, then everything was quiet. Everything but a soft, almost inaudible sound from next door. I went to the door to listen and heard the quiet sobs. Gathering my voluminous duvet around me, I slowly opened the door.

"Are you alright?"

No sound.

"Are you frightened?"

A stifled sob.

Now I could see the small figure snuggled under the bedclothes, and felt a wave of tenderness and sorrow and compassion. I moved to the bed. She made room for me. I felt the unbelievable softness of that small body. She almost disappeared as she moved into my arms.

We lay still for a long time. It was so strange and so natural and so wonderful.

Once, she said, "Where is Yugoslavia?"

And much later, she said, "Are you really a high-ranking officer?"

I smiled and kissed her.

"Life is funny!" she said. A pause " - and sad..."

It was already getting light before either of us woke, but the spell was still there. We moved as in a dream as we washed and dressed. She produced an old-fashioned straight razor and I shaved as she lit the stove. When I came out, there was hot milk, two boiled eggs and bread and cheese. She drank some milk, but didn't eat. Instead, she watched me with her serious grey eyes.

When it was time to go, I took her in my arms. We stood a long time, just holding each other. Finally, she turned her face up to me and we kissed. When she moved away, I started to talk, but she put her fingers over my lips and shook her head.

"Geh!"

There was something so serious, so urgent, so desperate in that word "go", I stumbled through the farmyard to the lane.

Then I knew there was something I wanted to ask her. I turned, but the little figure was running away. There were tears in my eyes as I watched her go.

"Life is funny - and sad!"

I had wanted to ask her name.

*****

Chapter 5

NEVER THE SAME AGAIN

On the road to the west, it was the same sad parade as before. The refugees, the scattered groups of soldiers, the peasants sowing the seed and doing their chores as they always have, war or no war.

The towns and even villages showed signs of destruction. That night, I slept in the cellar of a bombed-out house. In the debris, I found a duvet and as I wrapped myself in it I could smell the stale sweat of the owners and wondered if they were dead or alive.

In the light of the next morning, I walked up the cellar stairs to what had once been the ground floor, but was now open to the sky. Private possessions were strewn about wildly. One corner of what had been a living room or the sacrosant front parlour was reasonably preserved. Photographs and portraits stared reproachfully from parts of the walls left standing. I felt glass crunch under my foot, and looked down at a broken photograph of a German soldier in the uniform of the First World War. He stared up at me with wide-open eyes.

"Don't blame me, brother!" I said.

In the front garden, there was more debris. I picked up a child's doll with one arm missing. I heard snatches of the lilting voice of my mother reading from Charles Kingsley's "The Water Babies":

"I once had a beautiful doll, dears,
The prettiest doll in the world;
Her cheeks were so red and so white, dears,
And her hair was so charmingly curled.
But I lost my poor little doll, dears,
As I played in the heath one day;
And I cried for her more than a week, dears,
But I never could find where she lay.
I found my dear little doll, dears,
As I played in the heath one day.
Folks say she is terribly changed, dears,
For her paint is all washed away,
And her arm trodden off by the cows, dears,
And her hair not the least bit curled.
Yet for old sakes' sake she is still, dears

The prettiest doll in the world."

I wandered out onto the road with the doll in my hand.

I suppose I had some idea of giving it to one of the children of the refugees, but as I walked along I began to notice people staring at me with sympathy, then quickly looking away as if embarrassed. I didn't know whether they saw me as a bereaved parent or a nut-case, but I realised it could be an advantage as I got closer to the combat area, where military checks would be stepped up.

The crump of artillery got louder and the number of low-flying fighters increased. I tried to see the markings on the familiar P-47s and P-51s I had flown so often and knew so well; but these were not the long-range fighters of the 8th Air Force. They were the tactical planes of the 9th Air Force, working with the ground forces to hit targets just ahead of the advancing infantry and armour whenever they called for a strike.

There were other signs that the front was close. There was a stream of wounded now, some in farm wagons, some in trucks, some on foot. The artillery was so close I could see flashes and smoke in the town ahead, followed by earth-shaking explosions. My map showed that this town was on a river and, according to Peter's calculations, on the other side of the river was the American army.

There was only one way to find out, and that was to keep on walking through the town. Soon I reached the outskirts. Even there, the destruction was bad, but as I got into what had been the centre of town, there wasn't a building that hadn't been hit, and most of them were completely destroyed. The main street dwindled into a winding path through piles of bricks and rubble cascading down from the ruins at the side of the street.

A military policeman stopped me.

"Combat area. No civilians. It's too dangerous."

"I'm a soldier on leave. This is my home. The Fuehrer says no retreat. I stay here."

I slurred my words to cover any foreign accent that might come through. It also fitted my shell-shocked appearance and the broken doll.

Another shell whined over and exploded ahead of us. The policeman shrugged and hurried on. I stumbled on through the rubble and ruins and finally came to the river.

The bridge had been blown and its stone abuttments and twisted girders protruded from the flowing water. The road led through the ruins of two towers and dropped crazily into the stream. An open area had been cleared. Facing what had been the approach to the bridge was a group of uniformed Hitler Youth, nervously grasping their weapons, which ranged from rifles to machine-pistols. Beside them was a motley group of uniformed soldiers and civilian volunteers. Some had guns, some seemed to have only hand-grenades. All were tense as they stared across the river.

Behind them, dug into the rubble, was an obviously well-organised and professional contingent of helmeted infantrymen. Some were entrenched around two 88mm guns. Others were in machine-gun nests. All were relaxed and seemed fully in control of the situation. This was the SS.

There was no way I could cross the river at this point, but I figured there weren't enough German troops to cover the entire length of the river bank. I turned aside through the rubble and picked my way along what had once been a side street. Away from the river, it was like a ghost-town, and no-one stopped me.

Finally, I came to the edge of the town and struck off into the countryside. It was now getting dark. Any activity seemed to be at the edge of the river.

When it was quite dark, I cut across a field towards the river. I watched the ploughed furrows closely to make sure they hadn't been disturbed by any mine-laying. I came to a road and crouched in the ditch. On the other side of the road was a line of trees and shrubbery which must be the river bank. There was some movement on the road. Foot patrols, motor-cycles and the occasional car went by. They moved slowly in the dark, their blacked-out headlights showing only a chink of light.

I waited until there was a lull in the traffic, then slipped across and crouched in the ditch on the other side of the road. Now I was sure the river was on the other side of the line of trees, but there was a short stretch of pasture to cross, and there were voices on the river bank.

I thought the field might well be mined. I moved along the ditch until I came to a fence, then followed the fence towards the river. Soon I saw the river itself. There seemed to be a raised path along the bank. I moved closer, stopped, and held my breath to listen.

Sure enough, I heard the sound of regular footsteps and soon a helmeted guard came into sight, carrying his machine-pistol at the ready. When he had passed, I crawled up to the path and peered across at the river. The bank was fairly steep, which would make mine-laying difficult. Besides, the rapid advance of the American army wouldn't have given them time to lay minefields, even if they had the mines available.

I decided there was no alternative but to take the chance. I slipped over the path and slid down the bank. The water was cold as I went in up to my waist. I took off my suit jacket and reached down into the water to undo my boots. As soon as they were off, I quietly pushed off into the swiftly-flowing stream. I had intended to avoid any splashing by using a discreet breast-stroke, but the spring water was cold and the current was swifter than I thought. I was being carried downriver, but making no progress towards the far bank.

And that bank, so near and yet so far, meant freedom, the end of the war, and home. I struck out, using the crawl regardless of any splashing.

Almost immediately, I heard the rattle of machineguns. I dived and swam under water until my head ached and I thought my lungs would burst. When I had to come up for breath, I was still not halfway across. I heard shouts on the bank behind me and, just as I dived under again, the deadly staccato rattle was repeated. They were calculating how the current would carry me and following me down-river.

I couldn't stay under so long this time, but when I came up for air I was in the darker water shadowed by the trees on the far bank. I couldn't dive again, and started to swim as silently as possible. There were shouts behind me and two bursts of firing, but the spurts of water where they hit were off to my right. They couldn't see me. I'd made it!

Soon, I was crouched in the mud of the other bank and started to clamber out. Then I was challenged by an American voice.

"Who goes there?"

I peered up the bank and saw the barrels of four rifles pointing at me.

"I'm an escaping American Pow!" I gasped.

"Oh yeah! Then why were you shooting at us?"

"I wasn't shooting! I was in the water! They were shooting at me!"

"He talks like an American," said another voice.

"That don't mean a thing!" said the first voice.

"At least let me get up the bank - then you can take me prisoner if you like!"

"Keep him covered!"

I crawled slowly up the muddy bank. When I got to the top, a rifle barrel was jabbed into my chest. Beyond it, I could see an American helmet, and under that a boyish American face. I rolled over on my back and laughed.

"Boy, am I glad to see you guys! Where are you from?"

The young face trying to look so tough suddenly softened.

"Cincinatti!" he said with pride. "Do you know it?"

"Sure!" I said. "I remember Cincinatti. There was a bar there called the 'Cat and Fiddle'. I remember Covington, too, across the river in Kentucky, where they didn't have the Sunday Blue Laws, so you could get a drink."

That did it. They lowered their guns and I got up and threw my arms around them. The months of fear and frustration were over. I was free. I was alive. I was home!

"I have to talk to your C.O." I said. "It's important."

They led me through what had once been a quiet German village, but was now more like the County Fairground after the fair was over.

There were still a few dazed civilians moving about like zombies, but they were lost in the crowd of American soldiers. They were everywhere. Some had apparently taken over the houses. Others, either drunk or exhausted, were lying beside the road or in the little gardens.

The whole scene was one of confusion and disorder. Some houses had been damaged, but even those which were intact had trampled gardens and broken fences, with much of their contents spilled out of the doors and windows. I had expected a neat, disciplined army. This was a sloppy rabble.

Bottles and booze seemed to be everywhere, and even those who had some duties were going about them in the most casual manner. I had thought we looked like tramps in our bits and pieces of uniform in prison-camp, but at least we had been clean-shaven and neat. Most of this lot had obviously not shaved for days and seemed to be wearing any combination of uniform they chose. Some were encumbered with rifles, pistols, automatics and even hand grenades; others were festooned with shoulder bags which presumably contained food or some other loot.

"How long have you been here?" I asked.

"Well, we just got here. They've been pushing us pretty hard. Only time we get to rest up a bit is when we hit a river!"

I began to realise that what I was seeing was the infantryman's war, a weary war, a dirty war. This was not the battle of chivalrous adversaries, masters of their own destinies, jousting with one another in the high, clean air. No room for heroics and bullshit here. This was the shit without the bull; the stench of the trenches as in 1914-18; the stench of bodies, alive and dead; the senseless, endless marching; the senseless endless slaughter; the senseless, endless sacrifice; the sheer bloody unfairness of it all.

We reached the road which led to the river, where the bridge had been blown. Here there were tanks stopped in the road and, near the head of the column, a jeep, in the back of which two officers were chatting. One was a full colonel and one a major. They were smoking cigars.

As we approached, the colonel took a swig from a bottle of whisky and passed it to the major. They had a map spread out between them, to which they turned their attention between slugs of whisky. I saluted and introduced myself.

"Major Goodson reporting, sir, escaped prisoner-of-war."

They both looked up without much interest. The colonel returned my salute with a kind of wave and offered the whisky bottle.

"Here, Major, have a drink!"

He spoke with a strong Southern accent which fitted in with his relaxed friendliness. I thought of the saying, "Let me talk to a soldier and I'll tell you what the General is like," and wondered if the casual attitude of his command was a reflection of their General's character.

Perhaps he read my thoughts.

"We're a little disorganised right now. We've been going like hell for the last few days - no sleep, and not much food."

"Colonel," I said, "I escaped on orders from the Senior American Officer of Stalag Luft III, now at Moosburg. The camp contains some three thousand Air Force officers, including many senior officers. We have reason to believe that the Nazis are planning to take at least some of these officers with them into the Redoute in the mountains north of Salzburg and use them as hostages."

The Colonel shifted his cigar from one side of his mouth to the other, bent over his map and jabbed his finger at a number of red circles.

"Yeah! We've got them marked. This one here is Moosburg. This one here is Dachau. We reckon they may need help faster there, if any of them are left alive."

I looked at the markings on the map, and then at the Colonel.

"I see you're well-informed sir, but could I suggest you approach the camp from the south and east to prevent them moving any prisoners?"

"Well, we have to rest up here till the engineers get a bridge across this little ol' river. Now, Major Simpson here is heading south to the main road to Munich. That'll take him round the river, then he can head back up north through Dachau to Moosburg. We poor bastards are going to have to string along on foot, and catch you up later."

"I would very much appreciate being able to go along with the major.

I have a duty to get back to my command as I promised."

"Can you speak good German?" asked the major.

"Yes."

"Let's go!"

"Just a minute," said the Colonel. "When did you last eat?"

I was so surprised at his concern I didn't answer right away. Besides, I couldn't quite remember.

"Better feed him, Major. I'm going to sack out."

I began to realise that under the exaggerated casualness of these troops there was a genuine concern for people and, above all, a no-frills efficiency that got things done with the least amount of fuss.

It had been the same in our Group, but I had thought we were unique. We'd been through a lot together and besides, when your wingman yells at you "Break right, Goody! Two 109s coming in on you!" you don't give him hell for not saying "sir". Maybe a year as a PoW, dealing daily with the stiff German command and even trying to keep up standards of discipline in the camp, had made me forget how fast combat brings one down to earth.

I was well fed, kitted out in Army uniform, and allotted a seat in a jeep, which joined the motorised and armoured Tank Force heading for Dachau and Moosburg.

At first, everything seemed to be in confusion. Even the officers didn't seem to know what other units were doing. I was used to leading fighter squadrons on missions in which targets, routes, rendezvous and almost every detail was planned well in advance and timed to the minute, and every pilot knew his place in the mission. Here, when I asked what was going on, the reply was a laugh or a breezy "Damned if I know!"

But as we rolled through the Bavarian countryside, I sensed that there was an organisation behind the chaos and that, somehow, everyone seemed to know what he had to do, even if he didn't know - and perhaps didn't even care - what the grand strategy might be.

One strategy, however, was very obvious at all levels - MOVE!

Nothing was allowed to hold up the rapid advance. At times, it seemed more of a race. If a vehicle broke down, it was towed out of the way to let others rush through. Military Police directed traffic through villages, towns and bottlenecks with violently-waving arms, shrill whistle blasts and raucous yells of "Move it!"

There seemed to be no organised resistance. The local people stared at the mass of men and machines which had suddenly invaded their countryside with a sort of dazed wonder. The few pockets of determined last-ditch resistance were either by-passed, overrun by heavy tanks, or blown to bits by the Tactical Air Force fighter planes which were constantly hovering above and could be called down at a moment's notice to blast enemy strongpoints, vehicles or troops.

I will always remember one typical scene. An SS defensive position had been blown apart by air strikes and there was no movement among the green-uniformed bodies scattered around like rag dolls. A group of about ten Hitler Youth, led by a boy commander, came running up to take over the position. They threw themselves down behind what was left of the sandbag defences and opened fire on the approaching tanks. The mass of armour rumbled inexorably forward, completely ignoring the brave little band.

Gradually, their fire petered out as their ammunition was expended. At this point, their young commander leaped over the sandbags, brandishing his gun, and ran towards one of the leading tanks. He stopped a few yards away and fired the last of his ammunition at it. The tank still rumbled on. For a moment, the boy stood still. Then he threw his empty gun at the great tank and broke down and sobbed as if his heart would break. He must have been about thirteen.

As we approached Dachau, I remembered that I had once been taken there from Moosburg, which was a subsidiary camp, to discuss some administrative matter with the German headquarters personnel. We had heard rumours of gas chambers in Dachau, so I had been particularly observant, but seen nothing to make me suspicious. It's true I was only in the Vorlager and had only seen the barracks from a distance, but they looked exactly like ours in Moosburg. It seemed inconceivable to me that anything like mass murder could have been perpetrated so close to a typical Bavarian town like Dachau, which probably had a population of close to twenty thousand decent people.

What is more, when the Swiss representatives of the "Protecting Power" had visited our camp, I had brought up the subject with them. They had dismissed me out of hand for spreading vicious rumours. I wish they had been with me went I went through Dachau just after the liberation; but I doubt if they would have had the gall.

And I wish I hadn't been there. I had thought that nothing to do with war or death could shake me anymore. But this wasn't war, or death, or anything else anyone had ever imagined. I knew I would never, ever, be the same again. I've learned to live with it, but it's always there and always will be, a sort of dull ache.

Even now, I find it difficult to write about it rationally or to try to describe it. But there are fragments which I can't forget, because they are part of a recurring nightmare.

I am standing within the blank walls of the gas chamber, but it isn't empty, as it is now. It is crowded. It is jammed. Men, women and children are struggling against being crushed. The great steel doors clang shut. The hissing of the gas is drowned out by the moaning, the sobbing, the crying. They are clawing at the doors, at the walls, at each other. The mothers can no longer hold up their children. They clasp them close and sink into the seething, moaning mass. The writhing, scratching, wailing, praying reaches a crescendo and then slowly subsides, until there are only moans, whimpers, sighs - and then silence.

And I am smothered under the mass of dead. And I am dead, too.

Now the bodies are cold and twisted into awkward positions, and stiff limbs stick out at odd angles. They are all naked and the gold fillings have been wrenched from their teeth and they are beginning to rot and smell. And I am one of them.

And there are thousands of them, tens of thousands. The stench gets stronger until I am retching, although I know I'm dead.

There are flashes of silent scenes. Piles of womens' hair, mounds of false teeth, the pathetic collection of personal belongings, tens of thousands of pairs of spectacles, each one sadly empty.

These nightmares are the pale reflection of the horrors which the mind refuses to contemplate, just as it did on that beautiful Spring morning in Dachau. But I remember also the GIs. Some wept; some swore; some turned away in horror; most vomited. They had been kids a few minutes before. They would never be the same again.

We had pinpointed the PoW and concentration camps in the area and now we headed for Moosburg. There was little opposition. The few pockets of resistance were simply by-passed and left to be mopped up by the infantry who were following behind us.

The speed of the advance amazed me. The distance that had taken me three long days to cover took less than a day, and in the late afternoon, we wheeled into Moosburg.

Everything was already in confusion. The camp gates had been flung open and Kriegies were sitting around, embracing any of their liberators they could find; laughing or crying or staring dumbly, not daring to believe it was true.

The combat vehicles of the spearhead had wheeled into the Vorlager to round up the German garrison. There was no resistance. They had been waiting for this for some time and they gave themselves up with a sense of resigned relief.

As we drove up, a figure detached itself from the group of grey-uniformed guards and ran towards me. It was Popeye. As he ran, he shouted, "Major Goodson, may I surrender to you?"

He began to pull his pistol from its holster. Immediately, the shots rang out. The small grey figure crumpled to the ground. I leaped from the jeep and ran to him. He was still alive and I cradled him in my arms like a child. The soldiers crowded round. They couldn't understand. Even the Major was baffled.

"What the hell is this? This is one of the bastards that kept you in this hell-hole! I don't get it!"

I looked up at the Major, but I couldn't see him for the tears in my eyes. What I did see was that same grey figure, cradling an American officer in his arms, as I was cradling him. I saw 2000 officers saluting their Popeye, as the strains of the Westfalen-lied brought a tear to his one eye. I saw that small grey figure rushing between me and the German guard to protect me from machine-gun fire.

Major Simpson was waiting for an answer. I opened my mouth, but no sound came. I shook my head and turned back to Popeye.

The medics came, took him out of my arms and carried him away. On the ground, I saw the pistol he had wanted to hand over to me as a sign of surrender. As I picked it up, a U.S. Intelligence Officer with a clipboard came up.

"That's U.S. Military property now. I'll take it."

The war was over. It was what the Germans called the "Zusammenbruch", the breakdown, the complete collapse. The scene in Moosburg was like a scene in a madhouse in a very bad play. It was not one scene, but a hundred scenes.

A wild-eyed S.S. Standartenfuehrer was marching up and down, giving the Nazi salute and declaiming Nazi slogans, mixed with gibberish. He was shouting one moment and crying the next. He was the King Lear of the piece. He had simply gone mad.

Nearby, U.S. Army soldiers were loading German officers into a truck to go for interrogation. One of them just stood there, staring, oblivious to the proddings of the soldiers. A German sergeant came up and took him by the arm like a child.

"You must get into the truck, Herr Hauptmann."

The Captain turned to him in bewilderment. The tears ran down his face as he asked, "Was it all lies, then? All lies?"

"Yes, Herr Hauptmann," the sergeant replied softly. "All lies!"

And he guided him gently into the truck.

A distraught woman came up and grabbed my arm.

"Major Goodson! You knew my husband! He was a good Kommandant! Tell them he did nothing wrong! He knew nothing about the gas-chambers of Dachau! Tell them!"

"I'll tell them he did his duty as well as possible. As for Dachau - he knew!"

Going home! Two words that even in the early days of the war had meant so much, but came to mean more and more as misery and fear grew through the years of combat and reached a peak during the drabness and despair of prison camp. The dream which for years I hadn't dared to believe in had come true. I could simply relax, wait for the necessary orders to be cut and return to that dream-world of luxury and all things great, the good old U S of A!

Of course, the war wasn't over. What many Americans thought of as their most serious war was still going on in the Pacific and there still seemed to be a lot of island-hopping to be done before the final fall of Japan.

After more than four years of constant combat and almost another year in prison camp, the prospect of a hero's reception in the U.S. and rest and recuperation, followed by training on jet fighters and command of a combat unit in the Pacific was the answer to all my prayers.

General Vannaman, Colonel Spivey and most of the more senior officers had been spirited away long before and there was nothing to stop me from leaving; nothing except a quick visit to make sure the Gegners were O.K.

I called at their flat. It seemed like years instead of days since I had hidden there like a hunted animal. Helga came to the door. She was glad to see me and of course I had brought some Nescafe - after cigarettes, the most valuable commodity in Germany.

Helga told me over coffee that Peter and Professor Schmidt had left some days ago to join the Freedom Movement in Munich, to take part in the 'revolution' which was to take over the city and deliver it to the advancing American forces. All Helga had heard was that their little band had faced more opposition, and found less support, than they had expected. By the time the Americans arrived, not many of them were left alive.

I promised to go to Munich and try to contact Peter, and get back in touch with her.

In Munich, things were still in confusion. Sometimes it was more difficult to mop up all pockets of resistance in the cities. In the open country, the ever-present umbrella of tactical aircraft could swoop down at a moment's notice and blast away any opposition. Artillery, tanks and infantry could complete the process of annihilation. In the built-up areas, it was more difficult. The last-ditch fanatical fighters of the Third Reich could hole up in houses, cellars and sewers until the onslaught was over and still emerge ready to fight on. The fact that by this time, no amount of heroic resistance could have the slightest effect on the final outcome didn't seem to deter the fanatics.

It was the German fascination for extremes: "Wenn schon, denn schon";

all or nothing. But the time of miracles was over and spirit and determination could no longer stem the flood of men and machines which flowed over them. If some of them were able to survive the successive attacks of air force, artillery and army, they were simply by-passed, and finally engulfed.

Gegner's band of anti-Nazis had indeed raised their freedom banner and attacked the German troops preparing to defend the city against the advancing American army. They had expected most of the civilian population and many of the German troops to rally to their cause, if only to prevent further destruction of Munich and more useless loss of life.

But they underestimated the discipline of the troops, stiffened by the fanaticism of the SS, and the mixture of patriotism and apathy of the civilians. They took heavy casualties, but there were still a number of survivors, including Peter Gegner and Doctor Schmidt, to welcome the US troops when they entered the city.

Helga, of course, couldn't understand why the Americans didn't greet her husband as an heroic ally. By the time they got to Munich, however, the problem for the advancing troops was getting supplies fast enough to enable them to continue their race eastwards, and there was no system for processing Germans trying to join forces with them.

So it was that, when I finally traced them, they were in an American PoW compound.

I would like to think that my intervention speeded up their liberation, but I doubt it. It wasn't that there was any tangible resistance to releasing them, it was just that no-one was interested enough to buck the system. And, of course, as the few sympathetic officials pointed out, the prison camps were crowded and primitive and the food minimal, but the prisoners were probably better off, at least physically, than if they were free; free to try to scratch an existence in an environment in which any and every fibre of the economy had been destroyed.

So it was some time before I was able to cut through the red tape and non-fraternisation rules to see my old loyal and brave friends.

We were in the Professor's one-room apartment in a relatively undamaged suburb of Munich. Schmidt and Peter, both much thinner, relived their moments of glory during the uprising of their freedom movement. They recognised that their heroic stand and the sacrifice of their friends who were killed didn't make much difference to the outcome of the war; nor did it lead to a spontaneous outbreak of anti-Nazi liberal sentiment which could have immediately started the formation of a German Democractic party, strongly backed by the Allies, which is what they had hoped for.

Peter blamed years of Nazi brain-washing for the apathy of the average German. Schmidt was probably closer to the truth when he said, "The heroes are weary - they're just tired out."

"At least we showed the world that there WAS a German resistance movement, and that was our main aim!" Peter said earnestly. I wondered if anyone gave a damn. I didn't say anything.

I had brought some whisky and before Peter left for home we had a final drink. He left with my best wishes and something more valuable in the form of coffee, cigarettes and food. I turned to Schmidt.

"Do you have a minute?"

"I have the rest of my life!" he smiled, and waved me to a chair.

"Professor - may I call you Klaus?"

"Please do!" he said.

I poured us both another whisky and raised my glass to him. His old clothes hung untidily on what had once been a bulky frame, but he looked more at home in them than he had in his soldier's uniform.

"Klaus," I said, "I've talked to a lot of Germans, during the war and since. I've studied the history of the Third Reich. I've seen the death camps. I've tried to understand. I'm still confused."

"I'm not surprised," he said.

"You are the only German I know who was opposed to National Socialism from the start and lived through the whole extraordinary drama of the Third Reich."

"What's your question?" he asked.

"Well, one question has to be: how could the intelligent majority give such fanatical loyalty to Hitler and his gang? Did they believe the blatant lies of Hitler and Goebbels?"

"One important factor is that people, whatever their nationality, basically believe what they want to believe. So when the German people were told that they were responsible for the First World War, they didn't believe it. When they were told they deserved the punishment inflicted on them by the Treaty of Versaillles and the resultant wild inflation and desperate poverty, they didn't believe it. But when Hitler told them that these sufferings were unjustly imposed upon a fine, superior race by their foreign enemies and international Jewry, they believed it!"

"But they knew that Hitler started the war by invading Poland for no good reason, other than greed!"

"You're missing the whole point. Hitler may have attacked various countries, but it was made clear to everyone, particularly the armed forces, that Germany had no basic argument with England, France, Belgium, Holland, Norway, even Poland, and certainly not with the United States. There was only one enemy, and that was Bolshevism; all the others were purely incidental. From the very beginning of the Nazi movement, they presented themselves as the only hope of preventing a Communist takeover of Germany.

"And they may have been right. At the beginning of the 1920s, there was every likelihood that the Communists in Germany would take over. They exploited the hopeless inflation, unemployment and poverty and were strongly backed by the Bolshevik government in Russia, dedicated to aggressive extension of communism throughout the world. Even those who may not have believed that Poland was planning to invade Germany realised that Germany would be much better off with a buffer state on its eastern border."

"That's ridiculous!" I said.

"Maybe, but you asked me how the Germans could back Hitler, and I'm trying to tell you. Mind you, I'm an expert - I've been studying it and puzzling over it for years!"

"And coming up with a nice excuse for everything!"

"Oh no," he said. "I don't excuse anything - least of all myself. After all, I was a student of political history and economics. I knew better! The others were swept along with it. They were sincere. They believed it all. I don't mean the fanatics, or the hangers-on, or the bloodsuckers. I mean the mass of ordinary, decent Germans.

"And look at them now, that dead look in their eyes, the stoop in their shoulders, the grey blankness of their faces: that's not just malnutrition or exhaustion after five years of war. That's the numbness of broken dreams, broken promises and broken spirits; the deadness of people who have sacrificed everything they had, everything they loved, for a cause and a leadership they believed to be glorious and just; only to find that the cause was false and vicious, the leadership sordid gangsters and mean murderers. Oh, they were gullible and stupid and maybe selfish, but they didn't deserve this!"

In translating Schmidt's words, I may have embroidered a little, but not much. This was the gist of it, and it made me mad.

"Yes, they feel sorry for themselves now, but they didn't have any pity for the millions who were dying in the concentration camps! Or are you going to pretend they didn't know?"

"Some knew, of course, but whether you believe it or not, they were surprisingly few - probably only those who were directly involved. And they had every reason to keep their deadly secret, even from their closest friends, and especially from their wives and families. The very enormity of the crimes ensured that those who knew kept quiet.

"Some didn't want to know. They may have had suspicions, but they had no real evidence and knew they could never come up with any real proof. More importantly, they didn't want to believe it - and remember, people believe what they want to believe. In any case, they knew there was nothing they could do about it.

"But the vast majority didn't know. Oh, they knew there were camps in which those who wished to take over the Government and the country for Communism were sent for re-education. They knew that these people had been joined by traitors and saboteurs. They knew that conditions in the camps were rough and tough, but that was what the enemies of the Reich deserved. Why should traitors eat as well as loyal Germans? Why should slackers not be forced to work for the Vaterland and for victory?

"As for the planned genocide of millions of people from all over Europe, simply because they were Jewish - no, they had not the remotest idea and many of them don't believe it even now."

"Well, I was locked away as a prisoner-of-war, yet I knew!"

"You told me that when you were in Moosburg you used to visit the camp in Dachau. The average German couldn't get anywhere near such camps. Even before you were shot down, you could have heard eye-witness stories from those few who had got out of the camps. You had a better opportunity to know than any German."

"I certainly didn't have a better opportunity than the citizens of Dachau! The camp was on the edge of town and there must have been a lot of contact between the town and the camp."

I wanted to get in the last word, but I was no longer so sure of my ground. It wasn't quite true that we had known about the gas chambers of Dachau. We had heard rumours, but wild rumours were rife in prison camp. Nevertheless, I had tried to do something about it by approaching the representatives of the International Red Cross and, more particularly, the Swiss Protecting Power. These neutrals were constantly visiting camps and making official reports on conditions in general and the treatment of prisoners in particular; yet, so far as I know, they never made any complaints about the horrors which later came to light.

In Moosburg on one occasion, I had been able to slip up beside a representative of the Swiss Protecting Power and hurriedly whisper in German that there were rumours about murders and gas chambers in Dachau. He looked startled, and stammered, "Je m'excuse. Je ne parle pas allemand."

I quickly repeated my message in French. He seemed relieved when a German officer separated us. In any case, nothing came of it.

So if those with the responsibility for investigating atrocities, with the right to search any camp, with no reason to fear the consequences, didn't know or didn't want to know, how could we state categorically that the average German knew, when they had no right and no opportunity to find out?

I poured another drink and changed the subject.

"Are you sure the average German is completely disillusioned with Nazism?"

"I don't know whether they are disillusioned or just plain tired of the whole thing and generally worn out. In any case, they don't give a damn any more. Their only concern now is survival."

"But they were enthusiastic enough right up to the end!"

Klaus laughed.

"You Americans - and the British - can never understand about German loyalty to the Nazi Government. You talk as if there was a choice. You seem to think we could have discarded Hitler and his gang and elected another party! We didn't have that luxury! There was only one Government and opposition to it was, by definition, treason to one's country. The Russians understood that better than you do, because they too have a dictatorship. They too have no choice!"

"There was a choice in the beginning. After all, Hitler was elected!"

"Not quite! Hitler did not become Chancellor following an election victory, but was engineered into power through the intrigues of conservative, rather than Nazi opponents of democracy, some two months after the previous general election had brought major losses in votes and seats for the Nazi party, and at a time when many thought Hitler and Naziism were finished. Hitler became the Head of Government by usurping the position. The only thing the German people were asked, and to which they gave a resounding answer, was whether they thought the Versailles treaty was wrong!"

"But he became popular!"

"Yes - because he promised to control inflation and unemployment, produce prosperity and, above all, get the Treaty of Versailles re-negotiated and restore German self-esteem and hope. What's more, he made good most of his promises!"

"I thought you were on the other side? When I first met you, Hitler and his crowd were the arch criminals to you, responsible for all the ills of the world. Now you seem to have changed your mind!"

"Oh, I don't think so. I believe I'm still devoted to the same ideal."

"And what's that? Neo-Nazism?"

"No - though it's just as unpopular right now. It's the same old search for the unvarnished truth."

"I don't understand," I said.

"No - that's the tragedy!" he replied.

***

I checked back into the motor transport centre in Munich and realised it might take some time to get a ride back to Landshut and catch a plane out. They were doing their best - and their best was pretty good, considering the confusion everywhere in the newly-liberated city.

A harassed Master-Sergeant wanted to help. "You got any priority, Major?"

"None whatsoever, Sergeant," I said.

"Just sit there awhile, sir, I'll see what I can do."

I was still sitting on a bench, staring at the general chaos, when I heard a hoarse whisper in my ear.

"Hey mister, you wanna jeep?"

I turned and looked into the mischievous, twinkling eyes of Willie. Willie had been a good friend of mine in prison camp. He knew everybody and everything. He was one of those people in whom other people confide. I've never been able to analyse this particular gift, but in Willie's case it may have been helped by his appearance. He was short and round, with the face of a comedian, and seemed to belong more in a clown's costume than in an officer's uniform.

He had been involved in the organisation of the secret radio in the camp and the distribution of the news. I remember thinking that the Army, typically, had miscast him as a humble pilot. He should have been involved in Intelligence and espionage. It was years later before I learned that he was.

"What the hell are you doing here, Willie?"

"I've volunteered for a stint of special duty before going back home."

"Doing what?"

"Oh, making sure all our Kriegies get out, including those liberated by the Russkis - stuff like that!"

I knew Willie was one of Nature's fixers, but his fixing was not always entirely altruistic.

"What's the racket?" I asked.

He looked hurt, then admitted, "Well, I was up for my Captaincy when I was shot down. By taking this job, I should get it. If I just went home, I might not!"

"But how did you fix it?"

"I have a few friends."

"Did you say you had transport? That's more to the point!"

"Sure, I've just picked up a jeep. Let's go!"

***

I had been assigned to a unit, re-issued with uniform and all other privileges of rank and given the task of helping to repatriate the American PoWs who had been liberated from the camps.

I was driving my jeep back to Munich after arranging for another group of ex-PoWs to be flown out of Landshut when the headlights lit up a female figure, struggling along at the side of the road with a large and obviously heavy suitcase. With the other hand, she was leading a small boy and trailing behind was a girl of about six, wrestling with a large parcel done up with string.

I stopped and offered a lift. The woman politely declined.

"You must be tired," I said, "and the suitcase looks heavy."

"No, thank you," she said.

I turned to the little girl. "You're tired, aren't you?"

Two big, soulful eyes gazed at me out of the thin face. She nodded. I got out of the jeep and slung first the battered old suitcase, then the brown paper parcel and then each child into the back of the jeep. I

On the corner of each Compound was a guard tower or "Goon Box", and these dominated the camp, with machine guns covering the forbidden alley between the fences. Two guards with field glasses constantly swept the area.

One of the compounds of Stalag Luft III before the overcrowding got too bad towards the end of the war.

Emptying the latrines was a constant and essential task. When rain and overcrowding caused the Aborts to overflow in Moosburg, it almost caused a riot. Only the timely arrival of the "Honey-Goon" averted a blood-bath.

The Memorial to the fifty officers killed after the Great Escape from Stalag Luft III, designed and built by their fellow-prisoners in the Military Cemetery at Sagan

The fifty prisoners who were shot after their recapture

To all Prisoners of War!

The escape from prison camps is no longer a sport!

Germany has always kept to the Hague Convention and only punished recaptured prisoners of war with minor disciplinary punishment.

Germany will still maintain these principles of international law.

But England has besides fighting at the front in an honest manner instituted an illegal warfare in non combat zones in the form of gangster commandos, terror bandits and sabotage troops even up to the frontiers of Germany.

They say in a captured secret and confidential English military pamphlet,

THE HANDBOOK OF MODERN IRREGULAR WARFARE:

". . . the days when we could practise the rules of sportsmanship are over. For the time being, every soldier must be a potential gangster and must be prepared to adopt their methods whenever necessary."

"The sphere of operations should always include the enemy's own country, any occupied territory, and in certain circumstances, such neutral countries as he is using as a source of supply."

England has with these instructions opened up a non military form of gangster war!

Germany is determined to safeguard her homeland, and especially her war industry and provisional centres for the fighting fronts. Therefore it has become necessary to create strictly forbidden zones, called death zones, in which all unauthorised trespassers will be immediately shot on sight.

Escaping prisoners of war, entering such death zones, will certainly lose their lives. They are therefore in constant danger of being mistaken for enemy agents or sabotage groups.

Urgent warning is given against making future escapes!

In plain English: Stay in the camp where you will be safe! Breaking out of it is now a damned dangerous act.

The chances of preserving your life are almost nil!

All police and military guards have been given the most strict orders to shoot on sight all suspected persons.

Escaping from prison camps has ceased to be a sport!

Soldiers of the British Commonwealth!

Soldiers of the United States of America!

The great Bolshevik offensive has now crossed the frontiers of Germany. The men in the Moscow Kremlin believe the way is open for the conquest of the Western world. This will certainly be the decisive battle for us. But it will also be the decisive battle for England, for the United States and for the maintenance of Western civilisation.

Or whatever today remains of it.

The events in the Baltic States, in Poland, Hungary and Greece are proof enough for us all to see the real program behind the mask of Moscow's socalled **"limited national aims"** and reveals to us how Moscow interprets democratic principles both for the countries she has conquered and also for Germany and **for your countries as well.**

It is also clear enough **today** that the issue at stake is not merely the destruction of Germany and the extermination of the German race. **The fate of your country too is at stake.** This means the fate of your wives, of your children, your home. It also means everything that make life livable, lovable and honorable for you.

Each one of you who has watched the development of Bolshevism throughout this war knows in his innermost heart the truth about Bolshevism. Therefore we are now addressing you as white men to other white men. This is not an appeal. At least we feel there is no alternative for any of us, who feels himself a citizen of our continent and our civilisation but to stop the red flood here and now.

Extraordinary events demand extraordinary measures and decisions. One of these decisions is now put up to you. We address ourselves to you regardless of your rank or of your nationality.

Soldiers! We are sure there are some amongst you who have recognized the danger of Bolshevik-Communism for his own country. We are sure that many of you have seen clearly what this war is now leading to. **We are sure that many of you see what the consequences of the destruction of Europe – not just of Germany but of Europe – will mean to your own country.** Therefore we want to make the following proposal to all of you.

We think that our fight has also become your fight. If there are some amongst you who are willing to take consequences and who are willing to join the ranks of the German soldiers who fight in this battle which will decide both the fate of Germany and the fate of your countries we should like to know it. We invite you to join our ranks and the tens of thousands of volunteers from the communist crushed and conquered nations of eastern Europe, which have had to choose between submission under an most brutal asiatic rule – or a national existence in the future under European ideas, many of which, of course are your own ideals.

Whether you are willing to fight in the front-line or in the service corps: we make you this solemn promise: Whoever as a soldier of his own nation is willing to join the common front for the common cause, will be freed immediately after the victory of the present offensive and can return to his own country via Switzerland.

All that we have to ask from you is the word of the gentleman not to fight directly or indirectly for the cause of Bolshivik-Communism so long as this war continues.

At this moment we do not ask you to think about Germany. We ask you to think about your own country, we ask you just to measure the chances which you and your people at home would have to, in case the Bolshivik-Communism onslaught should overpower Europe. We must and we will put an end to Bolshevism and we will achieve this under all circumstances. Please inform the convoy-officer of your decision and you will receive the privileges of our own men for we expect you to share their duty. This is something which surpasses all national bounderies. The world today is confronted by the fight of the east against the west. We ask you to think it over.

Are you for the culture of West or the barbaric asiatic East?

Make your decision now!

COPY.   20 June 1945.

SUBJECT: Commendation.

TO: The Adjutant General, War Department, Washington, D. C.

1. It is desired to commend Major James A. Goodson, A.C. 0-885241 for outstanding work while a prisoner of war at Stalag Luft III, Sagan, Germany.

2. Major Goodson devoted himself to the interests and welfare of Ps. O. W., contributing in a large measure to successful preservation of healthy minds and bodies of those in confinement.

3. Unusual handicaps had to be met and overcome. Living conditions were difficult, unhealthy and crowded. In spite of all these things Major Goodson laboured unceasingly to maintain the morals, discipline and comfort of his fellow prisoners.

4. Working with ultimate objective of salvaging all P.O.W. personnel in good condition and returning them to the service of their country, the staff of the camp, which included Major Goodson, was certainly successful as indicated by the fact that only one man was lost out of a compound of 2,000 officers and men.

5. It is requested that a copy of this letter be forwarded to the officer and included in his 201 file.

(signed) Delmar T. SPIVEY

Colonel, Air Corps.

Note.-Major James Goodson was Camp Adjutant in the Centre Compound for U.S.A.A.F. Ps.O.W. at Stalag Luft III at Sagan in Silesia, south of Berlin.

This Commendation was put in by Col. Delmar Spivey, who was the Senior Officer for all American Compounds for Ps.O.W. Goodson's 2,000 men were separated from Col. Spivey at Sprenburg when the forced marches began, and Jim had to take them under guard to Noosburg, Bavaria.

Scene of devastation in a German city. 1945

Following a raid, German civilians search the rubble.

A Mustang escorts a B-17 Flying Fortress

The Me-262

The Me-163 rocket plane

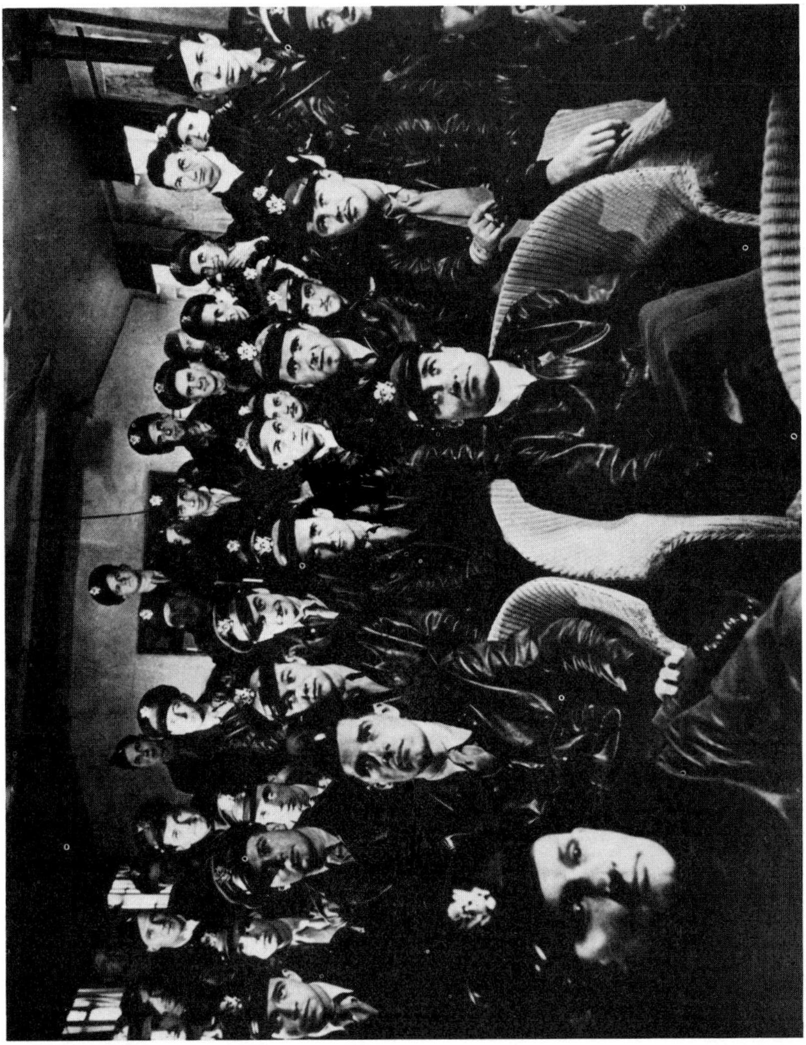

Macky Steinhoff

Guenther Rall

Gerhard Barkhorn

Hajo Herrmann

Pips Priller

Douglas Bader with his German captors

"Bubi" Hartmann

Adolf Galland

The Fighter Pilot Memorial erected to the fallen fighter pilots of WWII by the German Fighter Pilots' Association at Geisenheim.

Jim Goodson and Adolf Galland - no longer fighting, as represented on the cover of this book, but now old friends.

More old friends - L to R: Jim Goodson US, Guenther Rall Luftwaffe, Walter Krupinski Luftwaffe, Peter Townsend RAF, Hub Zemke US, Adolf Galland Luftwaffe, Geoffrey Page RAF.

Eagle Squadron Re-union, Colorado Springs 1989. "Snuffy" Smith, Jim Goodson, Lee Blakeslee, Don Blakeslee, Bob Wehrman.

Don Blakeslee, Steve Pisanos and Jim Goodson admire the model of Blakeslee's P-47 at the US Air Force Academy, Colorado Springs.

helped the woman into the front seat and started off.

"Where are you headed for?" I asked.

"Munich."

"Good - I can take you there. Where are you coming from?"

"The East!"

The reply could have meant that she was one of the many fleeing from the Russian-occupied zone and hoping to find refuge in the American area. In any case, it was obvious she didn't welcome my questions.

I turned to the children, sitting primly in the back, and offered them some chocolate.

"NO!" said the woman sternly.

"We mustn't!" said the little girl.

I didn't press it, but casually offered a cigarette to the woman.

"No, thank you!" she said.

I looked at the stern, sad face. She wore no make-up, her black hair was straight under a hat which might once have been fashionable but which, like her neat but shabby clothes, had seen better days.

I turned to the little girl, sensing that the offer of chocolate had won me some sympathy, forbidden though it was.

"Do you have somewhere to stay in Munich?"

"Tante Irma!"

"And does your Aunt Irma have children?"

"No - they're dead!"

I knew better than to ask Germans about fathers and husbands. The answer was almost always a shrug of the shoulders, or just one word: "Gefallen!" But I thought I was safe asking about the children. We, who had looked down a hundred times from above and seen the twinkling flashes and the mushrooming smoke, should have been able to translate them into indiscriminate death for men, women and children; but we never really did.

The woman was originally from Munich, and when I insisted on driving them to their destination, she was able to direct me. She explained that "Aunt Irma" was a friend who she hoped would put up her and the children until they could find accomodation.

That hope was quickly dashed as I helped them into the cellar of a bombed apartment block. There appeared to be only two main rooms. They were separated by a thin curtain, hung in an archway, and both seemed to be used indiscriminately by some seven adults, mostly women, and about ten children of various ages. And Tante Irma was very much in command.

All I wanted to do was to dump the bags and the kids and get out, but Irma was making it very clear, in strident tones, that there was no room and that the newcomers could not stay even five minutes. I'd wasted enough time on the sorrowful trio and in any case there was no way I could take on the overwhelming problems of the Germans, even if I wanted to.

I got into the jeep and drove off, but then realised I had to turn round to head in the other direction. As I swung round, the lights caught the three of them standing in front of the ruined building. The baby boy was rubbing his tired, tearful eyes with the back of his hand. The little girl held her mother's hand very tightly and looked up at her, almost as if to give her strength.

I swore loudly and jammed on the brakes. I fished out a PX bag from the jeep, got out and herded the little family back into the cellar. The woman Irma started her tirade again, but stopped in full flow when she saw the contents of my bag. There was simply some powdered milk, with a couple of cans of Nescafe and a few packs of American cigarettes; to the Germans in that cellar it represented real wealth. The atmosphere changed dramatically. The sudden silence was one of awe.

I gave Irma a pack of Camels, a princely sum in those days, and explained that it was to cover accomodation for the three for as long as they needed to stay. I gave my name and address to the mother of the kids and told her she could contact me if she had any problems. I then gave a chocolate bar to each of the children and a can of Nescafe, one of powdered milk and a bag of soap to the mother. She took it reluctantly and murmured an almost inaudible "Danke schoen!"

However, Tante Irma had swung into action. She ran towards the back room, pulled back the curtain and to cries of "Heraus! Heraus!" drove out an elderly couple and a few children. She then ceremoniously ushered the woman and I through the curtain.

I naively thought she wanted me to approve the accomodation. Even when she guided the children back into the other room and carefully drew the curtain closed, I didn't understand. Only when the noise in the other room dropped to whispers and I turned to the woman standing beside me did I realise what was so obvious to the others.

She turned to look at me. I had expected to see fear, anger or contempt. What I saw was worse. In the solemn eyes in the grey face there was only exhaustion and resignation. Tears started to stream down her face.

"I'm sorry!" she said dully.

I took out my handkerchief, handed it to her, tore back the curtain and strode back through the other room to the outer door. Irma, like the others, had been shocked into immobility by my sudden departure, but then she sprang up and tried to block my way out.

"Was ist los?" she wailed.

I pushed her aside roughly.

"But the coffee, and the cigarettes, and the soap..."

I realised the source of her anxiety. "Keep it!"

I started up the cellar steps.

"Alles - umsonst?"

Free of charge? For nothing? In vain? She couldn't even begin to understand.

"Ja," I said, "alles umsonst!"

*****

Chapter 6

WORSE THAN LOSING A BATTLE

I drove through the guardgate into the ex-German Army barracks where we were billeted and pulled up in front of the Officers' Mess.

In the bar, I was greeted by Willie. Without Willie, life would have been much less pleasant and our task of repatriating PoWs much more difficult. Today, his smile was broader than usual.

"I told you I'd get us out of this dump! Why don't you ever believe me?"

I was immediately suspicious. "Where are we going?"

"We're moving into a damn great schloss, that's where we're going! We move tomorrow!"

"How come we rate a castle?"

"Well," he admitted, "it's not exactly a castle, but it's a damn nice house, I've seen it and it's great. It's 'beschlagnahmt'. Some SS officer owned it."

The word "beschlagnahmt" was becoming very familiar to conqueror and conquered alike. It meant "commandeered" or "confiscated" and referred to German property taken over by the Allied forces. Property belonging to Nazis or war criminals was naturally taken over without compensation. Other desirable property could, and usually was, commandeered and a small payment made.

Our new accomodation was in the former category. It was a typically solid Bavarian house, probably built in the heyday of Bavaria in the 1880s. The main house stood in what could best be described as a small park, with trees and lawns rather than flowerbeds. Leading to the house was a gravelled drive, which swept round to a two-car garage which must once have been a stable.

When we arrived, a small detachment of military police was standing by whilst a striking-looking blonde woman supervised the departure of about fifteen adults and children. They were lined up, two by two, and started off down the drive. Last to go were an elderly couple. The blonde woman kissed them on each cheek and tried to console them.

"It's only for a while, you'll be back soon!"

The old man smiled sadly, shook his head, and went off with his wife to follow the others.

The blonde turned back, mounted the stone steps and turned to stand in the doorway of the house. I moved forward up the stairs until she barred my way.

"Excuse me," I said, saluting. She looked at me with disdain. Her eyes took in the pilot's wings and ribbons on my uniform.

"This is my home! It has many valuable paintings and antiques! Are you going to destroy it, as you have destroyed most of the beautiful buildings in Germany?"

"No, we'll take good care of your things. They are all listed in the inventory, but if you wish to take anything with you, I'm sure that would be alright."

"Take them with me? Where to? You have taken my home and have stolen or destroyed everything else in Germany!"

I was fast losing patience with this arrogant woman. I waved to the others to come in and we brushed her aside.

She was right about the house and its contents. There were Persian rugs on the parquet floors; heavy velvet curtains draped the high windows and excellent, if somewhat gloomy, paintings hung on the walls. Some of these were based on religious themes and dated back to the 16th and 17th centuries. As I walked around the rooms, I became aware that the woman was following me. I pointed to two 16th century paintings.

"They should be put into a gallery for safe-keeping."

"Why those two? They are all valuable!"

"No - not for the time being they're not."

This was the moment I had been waiting for.

"You see, the Nazis stole so many paintings throughout Europe, and although we are trying to restore them to their rightful owners, in most cases those owners were murdered by the Nazis. As a result, thousands of paintings of this kind are finding their way onto the market, and prices are therefore very low."

Her eyes burned with fury. She didn't speak, but her silence was eloquent. I walked away and continued my inspection of the house. Rooms were allocated and our gear was moved in.

I strolled into the garden. The beautiful trees had been preserved, but most of the lawns and flowerbeds had been given over to growing vegetables. I found a rather elderly character, who explained that he had been retained to continue his duties as gardener and janitor. The work was hard for him, he admitted, but it provided him with a room over the garage.

When I got back to the house, there was an argument going on. The woman was still there and refusing to leave.

"Does she have somewhere to go?" I asked the M.P. sergeant.

"Sir, maybe you could help me, you know, explain to her in German!"

I went over to her. "I understand you are not prepared to vacate these premises!"

"That is correct!"

I turned to the sergeant and said in English, "No problem! That Russian liaison unit wanted this place. We'll take their billets. It's closer to town, anyway!"

She caught the word "Russian" and repeated it, queryingly.

"Yes. It's not our policy to use force where we're not wanted. Our Russian allies have no such qualms. They'll be here shortly."

She looked at me with pure hatred, turned on her heel and started to walk down the drive. The sergeant looked surprised.

"Thank you, sir!"

"No problem!" I replied.

Halfway down the drive, she met the old gardener and said a few words to him. He came back to the house and emerged a few minutes later with two suitcases.

"What's that?" I asked him.

"The lady's things!"

"What's your name?"

"Helmut!"

"Helmut, could you sleep in the cellar of the big house, in the wine cellar?"

"Yes sir," he said in surprise.

"Take those bags to your room over the garage," I said, turning and going inside. From the front window, I watched her turn and slowly follow Helmut to the garage.

The next morning, I visited the vegetable garden. She came up to me.

"Where are your Russians?" she asked.

"They heard they would be confronted by you and retreated in confusion!" I replied.

"I suppose you expect me to thank you, but why should I thank you for allowing me to sleep in my own garage? Why should I thank you when it was you who destroyed our cities? How could you do it?"

"I guess we learned from what the Luftwaffe did to Warsaw, Rotterdam and London," I said, and walked back to the house.

Her imperious manner annoyed not only the enlisted men, but the officers. I returned one night to be informed that Frau Wolf wished to see me. When she arrived, I said, "Frau Wolf, you wished to see me?"

"I wish to make a formal complaint against the behaviour of your so-called officers and men. I am not allowed into the house to make sure my property is not being destroyed or stolen!"

"Frau Wolf, may I remind you that you are here under sufferance and can, and probably should, be moved out at any time? This property no longer belongs to you and you have no right to enter the house!"

"You have taken this house because my husband fought with honour and loyalty for his Fatherland and the Fuehrer, but my husband is now dead; and in any case, this house belongs to me and my family, and always has!"

"You know, you have to work that out with the German authorities, not with me. Under the non-fraternisation order, you should have no contact with any American military personnel."

"Do you think I want contact with your uncouth soldiers? It is they who offend me, with their swearing and bad manners. And the officers are just as bad! They have no culture, no manners, no breeding! As a German lady, I am used to German manners, not American boorishness!"

I tried to speak quietly without showing my fury.

"We have learned all about German manners in the concentration camps of Buchenwald, Auschwitz, Dachau and a hundred others. German manners have made you the most hated race in the world. I have seen the mountains of murdered men, women and children being bulldozed into mass graves. They had learned about German manners the hard way. Now get out!"

I opened the door, then slammed it shut behind her.

Some days later, I drove back from Landshut Air Base late at night. I swung into the drive and on into the garage. The large doors were open, so I didn't need to slow down but, as the headlights lit up the rear wall of the garage, I was confronted by an incredible scene.

A large SS officer in full uniform was standing against the wall three feet in front of me. In his hands was a sub-machinegun. For a moment, I was too surprised to move.

"Switch off! Engine and lights!"

He had the voice of a man used to giving orders - and to having them carried out. I didn't argue when he ordered me out of the jeep and pushed me towards the door in the rear corner of the garage. As we approached, it opened. I hadn't seen her in the dark, but of course she would have been there. I began to understand.

I was forced up the narrow staircase and into the small attic room. He made sure I was unarmed, then pushed me down into a chair.

"Major Wolf, I presume?"

I was acting much cooler than I felt. An SS officer on the run didn't have much to lose.

"Sturmbannfuehrer!" he corrected me.

"Sorry!"

I never could remember the names of equivalent ranks in the SS.

He sat down on a small settee opposite to me, covering me with the gun. She sat down beside him. He carried a pistol in a holster on his belt. She opened the flap, slipped out the gun, clicked off the safety catch and held the weapon in her lap, pointing at me. She was looking at me with hatred and determination. I knew she would pull the trigger without the slightest hesitation or regret.

I turned to look at her husband. He must have been close to Hitler's ideal of an SS officer; tall, broad-shouldered, handsome and obviously as tough as nails. Only in the darkness of his complexion and his black hair did he deviate slightly from the Aryan ideal. I looked into his face. There was not much expression, but a great deal of strength. He looked haggard but determined. I guessed he was not particularly intelligent, and certainly not imaginative but, perhaps because of that, he was the kind of officer I would choose to carry out a mission requiring complete commitment and unlimited courage.

His uniform was shabby, but carefully brushed. The boots were badly scuffed, but had been well cleaned. His face was suntanned, but was not unshaven; so he had been here for at least a few hours.

"I see that the rumour that you had been killed on the Eastern Front was a little premature?"

He wasn't amused.

"How did you get here?" I tried again.

This seemed to awaken a sense of pride in him.

"Fought our way through! From Vinogradov in the Ukraine, through Hungary, Czechoslovakia and Bavaria! Twenty-six of us hacked our way through a whole American division like a hot knife through butter!"

"Congratulations! Where's the rest of your unit?"

"We are waiting for them. They will be here in a few hours!"

"Good! Well, I don't want to intrude. I've had a busy day, so if you don't mind, I'll go to bed!"

"Oh no!" he said. "You are part of our plan. You will wait with us!"

"You mean I'm a hostage?"

"If you don't help us, yes!"

"Help you do what?"

"Continue the fight!"

I shook my head.

"You're mad! If ever there was a war that was fought to the bitter end, this was it. You Germans always do things one hundred per cent. You fight a war one hundred per cent. You lose a war one hundred per cent. And this one is finished one hundred per cent. You might as well accept it!"

"No!" he said. "It may take some time, but we will win! We MUST win! We are the only hope for the world! We stood against the Bolshevik menace. You and the British were too stupid to realise that, but you will learn! You will come crawling to us for help!"

"I think not. We will certainly be willing to work with Germany to build a new Europe, but it has to be a new Germany. You and your Nazi charade are finished and the world is so disgusted with you that they'll never allow you to start up again!"

"When you and the rest of the world get to know your Russian friends and their plans for world conquest, world enslavement, you'll realise how right we were and how wrong you were to stab us in the back!"

"You invaded Czechoslovakia, Poland, Norway, Denmark and Russia without even declaring war on them and, in the case of Russia, when you had signed a treaty of friendship and non-aggression; and you have the nerve to accuse others of stabbing you in the back?"

"We had to move fast to prevent others from invading first. You wear RAF wings. You must know England was planning to move into Norway. We only just got there first!"

"It started long before that. It started with the coming of Hitler. That was the end of justice and democracy!"

"You're right!" he shouted. "That was the end of what you call justice! The crippling terms of Versailles, which condemned Germany to poverty and made sure Germans could never claw their way out of it! You didn't see what you call justice at work in Germany. You didn't see the poverty and restrictions inflicted on the people of Germany. I can still remember, as a child, seeing my parents dressed in their shabby old clothes that were their best, carrying a cardboard box to the outskirts of town. In the box was the body of their baby, which had died of malnutrition. That was your justice!

"And that was democracy, too. Thanks to your trained fleas in the so-called 'democratic' Weimar Republic, we had every kind of indignity heaped upon us. We saw our money become worthless because of wild inflation. And because of the restrictions imposed on our country, there was no hope of ever working our way out of the mess. We saw our children and our children's children condemned to discrimination and poverty for ever. That was your justice! That was your democracy!"

There was no doubting the strength of his feeling.

"Then came the Fuehrer! Suddenly, almost overnight things changed. There was work, there was productivity, there was progress. Above all, there was hope!"

"Not much hope for the millions who disappeared into the concentration camps, never to be seen again," I said.

"Oh, there were many who wanted to see communism in Germany. They were backed by Bolsheviks and Jews, both inside and outside Germany. But Hitler was not going to allow our country to be dragged down to the level of the Soviets, or controlled by Jews and foreigners. The Fuehrer saved our country and stood as a bastion against the spread of communism!"

"Are you sure that all the babies and children who were starved and shot and gassed in the death camps were plotting a Bolshevik revolution?"

"That's enemy propaganda! I admit the concentration camps were not luxury hotels, but serious problems require drastic remedies. Enemies of the Reich had to be cut out like gangrene! At the end of the war, we could not get food through to them and that is when many died, but those who spread rumours about death camps and gas ovens are lying! They are trying to please the enemy and give them an excuse to murder the brave soldiers of the SS! They couldn't beat us when we could fight them, so now they want their revenge!"

I looked at him. He was obviously sincere.

"You are in the Waffen-SS. Maybe you weren't involved in the death camps, but if you've been on the Eastern front, you must have seen the Einsatz-kommandos massacreing thousands of prisoners of war and Russian civilians!"

"You are naive! You think fighting the Russians is like playing cricket! They never signed the Geneva Convention and never pretended to adhere to its rules. We soon learned they thought nothing of shooting prisoners of war. As to civilians shot, they were fanatical partisans, sabotaging and murdering - even killing their own people!

"I remember during the worst of the Russian winter, we came across a civilian train stopped on the steppes. The partisans had taken the engine, leaving the carriages with no heat. They had then smashed the windows, told the passengers they were to die because they hadn't continued to fight the German army after the Red Army had retreated. When we found them, only three were still alive. The others were frozen stiff!"

I felt it was time to change the conversation.

"How long are you going to wait here?"

"My men should be here any time now!"

"And then what?"

"We're going to fly out!"

"Where to?"

"We have friends."

"Well, I doubt if they'll appreciate you turning up in an SS uniform!"

"Unfortunately true, and that's one of the reasons for my being here."

He pointed to the small bed. On it was a civilian suit and a raincoat. He handed the gun to his wife.

"She can use it as well as I can - and wouldn't hesitate!"

"I'm sure you're right," I said.

He took the clothes and stepped through the door. I looked at the woman and shook my head.

"He hasn't a chance, you know. Can't you talk him out of it? If he gives himself up, he faces a little while as a PoW and de-Nazification and then he'd be free to start a new life."

Her face showed no expression as she stared back at me, but Wolf had heard what I said. As he came back through the door in civilian clothes, he answered me.

"Oh no! No freedom here for me! All your friends can't wait to bring me to trial, starting with the French!"

"What for?" I asked.

"For losing the war!"

"Nonsense!"

"Not nonsense!" he replied. "They accuse me of killing French Resistance leaders!"

"And didn't you?"

"I rounded up the leaders of the espionage and sabotage organisations, just as such people would be arrested in England, America or Russia. There was no doubt that they were guilty. That is freely admitted. In fact, they have been given medals for it. The death sentence for such subversive activities in wartime was accepted by the Geneva Convention and imposed by all countries, but that won't help me because we lost the war!"

There was real bitterness in his voice, but there was also tension. He looked at his watch, took the gun from his wife, keeping me covered, and sat down facing me again. He handled the gun with easy familiarity, but with deadly expertise.

He looked at his watch more and more frequently as the minutes passed and the tension mounted. Finally, Frau Wolf said, "They're not coming."

"No", he admitted, "but it doesn't matter. We planned for this possibility."

He stood up. "Come!" he said to me. "Get your pass out! You are going to drive me where I tell you. You are going to get us through all guard gates and patrols. I will have the gun in your side and if there is the slightest hitch, it will go off!"

The gun was already in my back as we went down the stairs to the garage. It stayed in my back as he embraced his wife and I heard whispering and a final, "It won't be for long! Till then!"

He pushed me into the garage and into the driving seat of the open jeep. As he got in beside me, he covered the gun with the raincoat he was carrying and pressed the barrel firmly into my ribs.

"You don't need to worry! After surviving four years of combat, I'm not going to risk my neck now! I keep telling you, the war is over, and you'd be a lot better off if you'd accept that!"

"Shut up!" he hissed, "and drive out!"

The house and driveway were in darkness. Normally, the street at the bottom of the drive was lit by street-lamps, but as we turned out of the drive I saw that they were not on and the only light came from the headlamps of the jeep.

"Let's go!" he said.

I slipped into top gear. Peering ahead, I thought I saw darker shadows against the dark trees, but I didn't slow down.

Then we were blinded as half-a-dozen searchlights came on. Hearing loud shouts of "Halt!" I jammed on the brakes. Wolf was thrown forward. I grabbed at the barrel of the gun and forced it forward. With all my strength, I held it pointed down under the dashboard. Helmeted khaki figures were rushing forward, but before they could reach us, Wolf wrenched the gun from my hands, stood up and aimed at the American soldiers.

"Drop your gun or I shoot!" I heard.

Almost simultaneously, there were flashes and shots and the German slumped forward over the windscreen. The gun was half under his body. I pulled it out. It was sticky and warm. It was also unloaded.

"You alright, Major?" The captain seemed to be in charge of the unit. I returned his salute.

"Thanks a lot! How did you know what was happening?"

"We've had the place under surveillance from the start. We knew he'd turn up here sooner or later, so long as his wife was here."

So that was it.

"Congratulations!" I said. I hoped it sounded sincere.

There was silence and I realised they were looking behind me. I knew she was there. I turned to face her, but she stared straight ahead as she advanced steadily towards the body in the jeep. As she reached it, the Captain moved forward to restrain her, but I waved him back.

She leaned over, took his head and shoulders and turned his face towards her. She put her hands around his neck, undid the clasp and drew out the Knights Cross on its ribbon. She laid his head back gently, made the sign of the Cross and walked back up the road.

From somewhere in the darkness, Willie appeared. He took my arm and started to lead me back to the house.

"What happens to her?" I asked.

"If you like, we could charge her with harbouring a criminal. It can carry the death sentence."

"And if we don't want to charge her?"

"I'll just tell her to get lost. I don't think they'll follow up on it. Even the eager beavers are getting tired of it now. Everyone just wants to go home. I'll tell her first thing in the morning."

"No," I said. "I'll tell her."

"You'd better get some sleep."

But I couldn't sleep. Sometime before dawn, I found myself walking towards the garage. At first, there was no answer to my knock. When she eventually opened the door, she was wearing a white silk dressing gown. Her long blonde hair hung almost to her waist.

She stared at me dully, uncomprehendingly. Then I saw the hatred, rage and fury building up until the dam suddenly burst. I felt her fists pummelling my head and face, her nails gouging my cheeks and eyes. When I raised an arm to ward off the blows, she bit deep into my wrist. At the same time, she screamed curses and accusations at me and the Allies, calling us murderers, liars and hypocrites.

The screaming gradually stopped as she gasped for breath, but her arms and legs kept flailing as she rained blows and kicks on me. If she had had a weapon, she would have killed me. As it was, her strength began to fail. She made one final effort, raising both fists to bring them down on my face.

My arms went round her waist, partly to stop the kicks and blows and partly to stop myself falling. Her strength gave out and her arms dropped around my neck; her legs gave way and her body was wracked by sobs. I got her to the narrow bed and laid her down. She clung desperately, the tears stinging my face where her nails had scratched me. I cradled her and tried to console her, as one would a child.

Gradually, the heaving sobs subsided. I looked down and gently brushed the tears from her face. Her large grey eyes opened. For the first time, there was no anger in them. They were the eyes of a frightened little girl.

"Where are you going?"

She was fully dressed and packed. She shrugged.

"What do you care? You don't need me anymore. You have got everything you wanted - and now the final victory! Bravo! You must be very proud of yourself!"

I stared at her. I couldn't believe it. But it was true. She meant it. I murmured to myself.

"What did you say?"

"Nothing except a battle lost can be half so melancholy as a battle won."

"Who said that?"

"Wellington, after Waterloo."

"Well, he would - he won!"

She opened the door, picked up her bags and left without a backward glance.

*****

Chapter 7

ILLEGAL ENTRY

"Willie," I said. "I'm going home."

"Why? There are no interesting assignments going. You'd be better off here for a while. There's still a lot to be done out here."

"No, there isn't. All the Allied prisoners are on their way home now and it was much easier than we thought. All that's happening now is that millions of Russians, Poles, Czechs, Hungarians, Yugoslavs and others are being handed over to a regime which is just as repressive as the one we're so proud of defeating. It must be the biggest sell-out in history!"

"Hell, the carve-up of Europe was agreed at Yalta while the war was still on! There's nothing you or I can do about it now!"

"Maybe not, but I don't want any part of it. I've flown with the Poles. They were the leading squadron during the Battle of Britain. My best friend was a Pole who got shot down on D-Day. They fought for our country, and we gave their country away to their ancient enemy. The Polish airmen who have gone back since the end of the war have never been heard of since.

"And how about the Cossacks and the old Russian emigres? You were as sick as I was when they were herded off to their deaths. My father died in 1921 fighting with the American, British and other Allied forces supporting those same White Russians!"

"Okay, there are always innocent victims of war. But those things are over and done with now. But you can still do a lot over here. We've got the great trials of war criminals coming up. You speak German and you've seen the war from both sides. Your experience could be very valuable!"

"Thanks - but we've seen who gets sentenced as war criminals; the leading aces of the Luftwaffe! I've fought them for years. They were rough, they were tough, but they never played it dirty. Their standards of chivalry were probably higher than ours. You know, when Goering asked Galland what he would do if he learned that one of his pilots had shot an Allied pilot in his parachute, Galland replied, "I'd have him court-martialled and shot!" And Goering replied, "I would have expected no other reply from one of my Generals!"

"I couldn't have answered for all of MY pilots, Willie. And yet we've turned some of the leading Luftwaffe aces over to life in the prison camps of Russia and are even keeping outstanding leaders like Galland and Priller locked up, in flagrant violation of the Geneva Convention!"

"O.K." said Willie. "So some things went wrong in the confusion at the end of the war! We weren't set up to handle all the problems. But now we're getting it organised. We'll separate the good guys from the bad by due process of law, and we'll have the world's leading lawyers and judges to administer it."

"Great!" I said. "But I don't want to have anything to do with it!"

"Why not? It would all be legal!"

"No! Legal is the one thing it won't be! It may be necessary. It may even be right. But legal it certainly isn't!"

"How come?"

"What law were the so-called War Criminals breaking? German law? Hitler was the law in Germany and they followed that to the letter. If they had defied Hitler, as we say they should have done, then they would have been breaking the law."

"What about international law?"

"What international law? The League of Nations made a few vague recommendations, but Germany wasn't allowed to be a member after the First World War, so how it could it be illegal for German nationals not to follow its recommendations?"

"Don't you think there should be any trials? Do you think those war criminals should go free?"

"No, but I don't think they should be tried by the Allies, their enemies, under some pretence of legality. They should be tried by Germans in German courts. They might get lighter sentences; they might get heavier sentences; but at least they'd get legal sentences. As it is, most Germans, guilty or innocent, will believe they're being tried because they lost the war!"

"Well, that's obviously not true!" said Willie.

"Are you sure, Willie?" I asked. "Where are the Allied accused? Did none of them do anything wrong? Are they being tried? No, only the losers are there. And to make sure nothing nasty comes out, they're going to rule out "Tu Quoque" as a defence."

"Rule out what?"

"Tu Quoque. It's a legal term meaning "you did the same". In the trials, it means for instance that when Generals Keitl and Jodl are accused of carrying out Hitler's orders to turn over certain categories of prisoner to the SS, knowing they would be sent to death or concentration camps, they will not be allowed to mention that British Generals and Americans carried out orders to turn over to the Russians those Poles they asked for - and a few thousand more for good measure - and White Russians and many others, knowing they would be sent to camps or death. And when they accuse Doenitz of telling his U-boat commanders not to stay and pick up survivors if that meant endangering their boat, he will not be allowed to use the evidence of Admiral Nimitz that he gave the same order to US submarine commanders."

"Well," sighed Willie, "I can't argue with you, but I wish you'd stay. I'll miss you. After all, your replacement might be even worse than you!"

"If an honest war breaks out again, Willie, I'll be back, but this kind of paper-pushing and nit-picking I can't stomach!"

"Coward!" he said.

I was to fly back to the States from England, and fly to England from Frankfurt. Since I had time, I arranged to drive a jeep to Frankfurt and instead of taking the autobahn I cut across country using the old Landstrasse, through the smaller towns and villages. I began to realise that I was in a different world, a world that seemed not to have been blighted by the war; the old world, the sane world, the world I had thought was dead.

Out in the fields, the farmers and their families were bringing in the harvest as they had for centuries. Many of the towns and villages were undamaged and looked much as they must have looked in the Middle Ages.

I took the old Romantische Strasse and marvelled at the ancient charm of Dinkelsbuhl and Feuchtwangen, until turning a corner, I looked up at the walls of Rothenburg ob der Tauber, sleeping in the sunshine as they had for over five hundred years. Within the walls, the perfectly preserved medieval town with its spotless winding streets and quaint old houses seemed unreal. On our aerial maps, there had been a red ring round Rothenburg, indicating it was not to be attacked. Now I understood why.

I've heard Rothenburg described as artificial, but how can something five hundred years old be artificial? I'd rather believe that Rothenburg was real, and that the prison camps and the grim ruins of war were artificial. There was nothing artificial about the names of the fallen on the War Memorial in the St. Jakob Kirche, where many names were the same, indicating that some families had lost all their sons.

All along the route, I admired the colourful window boxes; almost every house and cottage had its neat display of bright red and white geraniums or other cheerful flowers. It was more than just adornment of the houses; it was like a fierce gesture of defiance of the past and a symbol of hope for the future. At least, it was for me.

Feeling cheered by the sight of Rothenburg, I headed for Hanau on the Main River, where I wanted to visit Hingeley, an English friend who had taken on the daunting task of rebuilding the Dunlop tyre factory, which had been flattened by the bombing.

First, I stopped for lunch at the Europe Hotel. I knew that food, like everything else, was in desperately short supply, yet the hotel had an atmosphere of faded gentility that I could not resist. It had escaped the destruction of the rest of the city because it was on the outskirts, and what damage had been done had been patched up, cardboard or wood replacing the broken windowpanes. The linen tablecloths and napkins were sparkling white and crisp and the elderly waiter was dressed in black tailcoat, a starched shirt with a wing collar and wore spotless white gloves.

He showed me to a table by a window which still had its glass intact and waited for me to order. I was the only guest, and my presence was obviously an embarrassment to him.

For someone used to living on the US military economy, where we had our housing, food, even "Script" currency, a sudden encounter with the German economy came as a shock. The waiter didn't offer me a menu and I knew that what little food might be available would depend upon immediate payment and would be very limited if paid in D-marks. I could have used "Script" or greenback dollars, but that was strictly against the law and the waiter wouldn't dare to suggest such a thing to an American officer.

I leaned back and took a packet of Camels from my pocket. I didn't smoke cigarettes, but I put one in my mouth and said, as if it were a sudden afterthought, "I'm sorry! Do you smoke?" and offered him the pack.

He bowed, thanked me profusely and began to take out a cigarette.

"Keep the pack - it's finished."

Now I could order almost anything I liked, but I knew that such luxuries as meat would cause problems and take time. So I asked for soup, an omelette and a bottle of Mosel.

The waiter was obviously delighted and greatly relieved. He bowed, and backed away to the kitchen. I turned to look out of the window at the bombed buildings and piles of rubble just across the road. Suddenly, I saw the waiter rush across to the ruins, stop to roll up the bottoms of his trouser legs and tuck the ends of his tails into his belt, and take off across the rubble, leaping from one pile of bricks to another.

In a few minutes, I saw the grotesque figure come bounding back. In one hand, he grasped the four corners of a napkin which obviously held the eggs, and in the other he brandished a bottle of Mosel.

Almost immediately, he re-appeared in the dining room, now again transformed into the impeccable, dignified headwaiter, to present the bottle of wine for my approval. Only his heavy breathing confirmed that the strange creature I had seen bounding across the rubble had not been a figment of my imagination.

When I had finished my meal and was leaving, he reappeared with the packet of Camels. I had made a mistake, he said, the pack was not nearly empty and he could not accept so much.

"Let's say it was for the service, which was excellent!"

He drew himself up, his pride in himself and his profession rising above the dingy surroundings.

"In that case, sir, I should be honoured!"

I am told that, to this day, I still over-tip!

I made my way through the bombed city to what had once been the large Dunlop tyre factory. I found my friend Hingeley in his office in the partially re-built office section. The rest of the plant had been flattened, but to my surprise, there was a bustle of activity wherever I looked.

"What's going on out there?" I asked.

"Come on, I'll show you!"

They had got a patched-up boiler going. Under a makeshift shelter, an old Banbury mixer was clanking away and next to it they had put together a primitive calander to spread the rubber mixture onto the plies of fabric. Out in the open, some hundred men were straining to feed the plies onto simple tyre-building machines.

"What happens when it rains?" I asked.

"Oh, that doesn't bother them! It's the freezing weather and snow I'm worried about. I only hope we can get them some sort of cover by December."

"What's the problem?"

"No money! To prevent foreign speculators coming in and taking everything over, it is forbidden to bring in foreign capital. And of course there is very little local capital available even for the most essential basic investment."

"Then how did you get all this started?"

"Well, when I first arrived and faced all the old workers and managers, I thought 'My God! The poor devils think I've come here with a cheque-book and I have to tell them we can't invest a cent!' But they didn't worry when I told them that. All they wanted to know was whether I had the Vollmacht, the Power of Attorney which allowed me to sign for the company. Soon I was signing like mad, and things started happpening. My signature was enough to get our suppliers to deliver at least a little of the materials we needed, and the German banks have helped as much as they can.

"But most of the progress has been thanks to our own people. You see those men over there in the rubble? They are from the second shift, putting in extra time, helped by their wives and children, reclaiming the old bricks by cleaning them off, and picking out steel that can be used as girders. When we can afford some mortar and concrete, we'll get some rebuilding going."

"I suppose you pay them overtime?"

"Overtime!" he laughed. "We don't pay them at all!"

"None of them?"

"Not yet. After two month's work, we give each worker a bicycle tyre. That's worth a fortune, especially on the black market. We're getting payments in from contracts with the Army now. They're about the only customers who can pay cash, so I'm hoping to pay the people soon."

We went back to his makeshift office, where he served me tea which his secretary had made on an electric hot-plate in the corner. He didn't ask whether I wanted the tea - which I didn't - but he waved his arm and announced "Tea!" as if he had produced a minor miracle, adding with pride "We've got milk and sugar, too!"

I knew he couldn't conceive that anyone would turn it down.

"I think it's amazing, the way you're pulling yourselves up by your own bootstraps."

"Oh, it's not me. I told you, all I do is sign things. It's these people. You have to admire them, and it's not just here. I was still in the army, assigned to the Central Commisision when I attended a meeting in Frankfurt. The Burgermaster of Frankfurt, a first-class chap called Kolb, had had a survey done on the damage done to Frankfurt and the feasibility of rebuilding. The report was devastating.

"The water mains were all destroyed, the power plants were flattened, the rail network and the Main barge harbour were in ruins, the tons of debris would be almost impossible to remove, and so on. In fact, the Report concluded that to rebuild Frankfurt on its present site could well take a hundred years. And do you know what Kolb said? 'In that case, gentlemen, we must start immediately!'"

"Brave words, but can they make it?"

"If German industry survives the dismantlement programme, and I think it will, then look out! British industry will be bumbling along with obsolete German machinery added to their archaic plant, and German industry will be equipped with ultra-modern manufacturing technology. What's more, look at this!"

He tossed over to me a copy of the London "Times". Three of the leading news stories were about strikes and threatened union action in the motor, ship-building and other basic industries.

"What are they striking about?" I asked.

"The usual things - shorter working hours, higher wages, no introduction of productivity programmes or automation. You've seen what our Germans are prepared to do!"

I laughed.

"You sound as though you think the Germans might win the war after all!"

"Not the war, but the peace, and that's more important. You think I'm crazy? Come back and tell me that twenty years from now!"

I did come back. I didn't tell him anything.

***

It was a beautiful October day. For the pilot and co-pilot of the C-47 Dakota, it was a boring trip from Frankfurt to Manston, on the south-eastern tip of England. They must have wondered why I had insisted on a flight plan that took us over Northern France to St. Omer before turning north to England; and why I sat in the co-pilot's seat straining my eyes to pick out the airfield. I couldn't believe that it was less than a couple of years since I flew over those hornets' nests of the Luftwaffe.

After forty-five years, their names, Abbeville and St. Omer, still give me a twinge of excitement and nostalgia. The old Luftwaffe pilots tell me they feel the same way about Biggin Hill, Gravesend, North Weald,

Hawkinge and Manston.

"Can you take her down a little, Lieutenant?"

"Going down!"

He probably thought his steep diving turn would impress me, but my thoughts were of a dive that no clumsy transport plane could begin to copy.

I was following Don Blakeslee, my Group Commander, in a screaming dive which had left the rest of the squadron behind. I realised I had to try to catch Blakeslee or he would be on his own. I went into a vertical dive, glancing behind, every so often, but never losing sight of the leader.

I saw him pull out of his almost vertical dive to come up under two 190's. I pulled out of my dive as hard as I could to cut the corner, almost blacking out. He was closing on one of the 190's. I knew he wouldn't fire until the last moment. He admitted to being a poor shot. But he left it too late. They had spotted him, and flipped over onto their backs and dived away in their classic evasive manoeuvre. But Blakeslee was after them, and me after Blakeslee, and Wehrmann after me. It was Wehrmann's first mission as my wingman. I had told him it was a "milk-run".

Our speed had hardly slackened in the few seconds we had levelled off, and now I was diving vertically again. The speed was building up well over 500 mph as I tried to catch up, and the plane was shaking violently. We flashed through a squadron of Spitfires, but there was nothing they could do but watch. They could never follow us at our diving speeds.

Suddenly we were in the hornets' nest; there were 109's and 190's all around. We still had more diving speed, but I saw that Blakeslee's two 190's were easing out of their dive, and he was following them. At the same time, I saw three 190's screaming down on Blakeslee and cutting in behind him to take him off the tail of their two buddies. "Horseback Blue One to Horseback Leader; three coming in on you at 3 o'clock high. I'm trying to cut them off".

I tried to pull out of my thundering dive, but the controls were rigid. All my strength wouldn't move the stick and I knew I was in the so-called 'terminal' dive from which many P-47's pilots never were able to pull out. I dare not pull back on the throttle in case the nose went under in the start of an outside loop. I reached for the small winder that set the trim of the plane for take-off and landing, hoping that the little servo edge on the tail-plane would ease it up, but not fast enough to buckle the wings.

It worked. I blacked out, and felt as if my back was broken, but when my vision cleared I saw the 190's ahead of me, much closer, but still out of range. I was gaining on them thanks to the terrible speed I'd built up, but they were gaining on Blakeslee, and he was doggedly pursuing his prey.

I pressed my mike button. "Break, Horseback Leader, break hard right!".

It was just in time. Don broke into a tight right turn, but the 190's turned with him. We were well under 10,000 feet by now, where the FW190 could out-turn a Thunderbolt. But it gave me the chance to cut the corner, and zoom up under the last 190. He was intent on what was going on ahead of him and it was easy for me to close to where I could see the yellow nose and the black crosses on the fuselage and wings.

My first burst scored hits, so I gave him three more in quick succession. I was hitting him mostly around the starboard wing root. Suddenly there was a flash and a puff of smoke and his wing came fluttering off. The wing and the wildly spinning plane tumbled past me. I took a quick glance behind. Incredibly Wehrmann was still there, and I blessed him for it. There were other German planes above, but not dangerous - yet.

The danger was up ahead. Blakeslee was twisting and turning in a desperate effort to shake the leading 190 but the German was sticking with him like glue and he was scoring a few hits. The second FW was pulling up to close the trap on what he still must have thought was a lone Thunderbolt; but I was closing on him fast. My attention was on the lead German and Blakeslee in their deadly duel. "Hang on, Horseback, I'm gaining on him!".

I had plunged the stick forward to pick up more speed. Soon I was right under the second 190. I pulled up, laid off deflection aiming in front of his engine, and fired. I was too close to miss. The fire was concentrated. Flashes appeared on the engine and continued down the under-belly in four long bursts. The engine must have stopped, because I hurtled past him. The FW went straight into a vertical dive, trailing smoke, and exploded in a field not far below.

Now I could concentrate on taking the last 190 off Blakeslee's tail. "I'm coming up, Don, hang on!" He was too busy to answer. I wasn't quite in range. but I was gaining. Each second like an hour. I saw more flashes on Don's Thunderbolt. I had to try to hit his attacker even if I was out of range. I took careful aim and fired from dead astern. There were no hits. I tried two more bursts. Nothing. Then, on the fourth burst, I saw a flash!

"I've got him, Don!" I said.

"The hell you've got him. He's got me!" was Blakeslee's breathless reply.

Now I hit the 190 again, and was closing fast. He slewed around to see what was behind him, but then continued his attack on Blakeslee. He was either a very cool guy, or he mistook the two radial engine P-47's behind him for his own wingmen.

I pushed the firing button again to finish him off. There was the start of the juddering burst of the machine-guns, then a sudden silence. At first I couldn't figure it out; then I realised with a shock I was out of ammunition!

I looked back at Wehrmann, he was too far behind to be in range, and could never catch up in time. By now I was gaining fast on the 190, but he was still on Blakeslee's tail, and Don wasn't taking enough evasive action. Then I knew why.

"I can't see a damn thing! I'm covered in oil!"

I had to do something fast. I had no ammo, but I had speed, and was close behind the 190 now. I pushed the stick forward, dived under him, turned out to the side and up, to come up beside and a little ahead of him. I then turned straight into him. He must have been amazed to see a P-47 coming in on him at such close range, and the bluff worked. Probably almost by reflex action, he turned into the attack, rolled right on over, and split-essed for the deck. The ground was only a few hundred feet below us now, and I lost sight of him.

It was over, at least for the moment. It had seemed like a life-time, but the whole action had lasted less than five minutes.

I pulled up alongside Blakeslee. His canopy was wide open, his goggles were on, and at times he peered out from behind his windscreen which was completely covered by black oil. The whole fuselage was streaked with oil. The big white letters WD-C on the side of his plane were practically obliterated.

"Can you make it, Don?" I asked.

"I don't think so," he said. "Oil is spewing all over the place, and I have to keep the throttle wide open just to keep altitude. How far do we have to go? I don't even know where we are".

"We're about twenty miles from the coast and from there it's another thirty miles across the Channel". What I didn't mention was that we were almost in the traffic pattern of the Luftwaffe airfield of St.Omer.

I took a good look at his plane and said, "I think you'll make it. These jugs can absorb a lot of punishment. Steer five degrees further to the right".

That way he'd avoid Calais and its flak, and cross out between Calais and Gravelines, and he'd be heading straight for the long emergency-runway at Manston on the south-east tip of England. The bad news was that the heading would take us closer to St.Omer.

I was now weaving about and behind Blakeslee, straining my eyes to make sure no German fighters were following us out. The faithful Wehrmann had now caught up with us.

Suddenly I saw them. Two FW190's coming in low from the direction of St. Omer. They would probably have been able to see us from the ground. Quickly I turned to meet the two 190's before they could attack Blakeslee. Wehrmann was on my wing. As we attacked, the 190's broke and turned. That was good enough. I didn't think they would be able to catch us again from their low altitude before we were across the Channel. In any case number one priority was to protect Blakeslee. Also, I was really worried about fuel now; the needle was flicking against zero.

We swung back to catch up to Blakeslee again. Soon I saw the coast and picked out his plane just as he crossed out. We were pulling up to join him when I saw what I thought was another P-47 coming in at Blakeslee's level; but the next second, I knew the slim little stubby silhouette could only be an FW190. Once more Wehrmann and I wheeled down in a frontal attack; once more, he flipped over and dived for home. Once more we broke off and came back to escort our charge.

I pulled up alongside Blakeslee to lead him as straight as I could to the long Manston runway. It wasn't only that he had no forward visibility, but I thought there was a good chance he'd been hit in the hydraulics, which would mean no flaps and no brakes. He'd need all the runway he could get.

Right after leaving the French coast we saw those welcome white cliffs of Dover. I'd done a lot of flying over this tip of England, over which most of the Battle of Britain had been fought. Its airfields, Lympne, Hawkinge, West Malling and Manston had been home to me in the early days.

I heard Blakeslee say, "Where the hell are you taking me?"

We had passed Dover and I could see St Margaret's Bay on our left. "We're dead on course. The longest runway in England is about ten miles ahead of you. You can go straight in".

When we had passed Deal and were coming in over Pegwell Bay, I pulled out a Very pistol, pulled back my cockpit canopy, and shot off a red flare to make sure Manston was ready for an emergency landing. Ramsgate was on our right, Sandwich and its golf courses on our left and, dead ahead, the long runway.

"Drop your wheels, Don!" I was flying right on his wing now, and he was watching me, as I was watching him. Both of our undercarriages came down at the same time.

"OK! They're down".

I waited till I knew he could reach the end of the runway before saying;

"Flaps!"

I put mine down, and he started pulling ahead of me. No flaps!

"No problem, Don, we're in good shape!" I raised my flaps, caught up to him, eased back the throttle and flattened the approach.

"OK, Don, cut your throttle, you're almost on the end of the runway".

I was a few feet from the grass at the side of the runway. I opened the throttle, poured on the power, raised the wheels, pulled up to go around again, and prayed there was enough juice for a tight circuit. As I pulled around, I saw Wehrmann coming in on his approach. He probably had even less gas than I had.

I made a tight Spitfire circuit, dropped the Jug at the start of the runway, and let her roll down to the end where Blakeslee and Wehrmann had stopped. I pulled up beside them, cut the engine, and clambered out.

Blakeslee was walking around his plane inspecting the damage. Both of them were covered in black oil.

"You OK?" I asked.

"Yeah, but I don't know how they missed me. Look!"

The sturdy old P-47 was riddled all down one side. He turned to me.

"That was real good shooting".

"Thanks", I said.

"I don't mean you; I mean that bloody 190! What the hell took you so long? I though I'd had it!".

"Oh, I took the scenic route. Anyway, I knew the old bastard could take it", I said.

"Yeah!" he said patting the oil-streaked side of the P-47. "This old gal can sure take it!"

"I don't mean the plane; I mean you!"

I walked over to where Bob Wehrmann's plane had pulled up. He was still sitting in the cockpit in a daze. I climbed up on the wing, clapped him on the shoulder, and said,"Damn good! I don't know how you stayed with me!"

The sweat was still running down his face, as he said with feeling "Neither do I!"

"Thanks!" I said as I turned away.

He nodded, then called after me "Say, Goody, let me know when you're planning the next milk-run."

Blakeslee was looking over my plane. "Do you want to fly her back to Debden?" I asked.

"Not on your life! Do you know you've bent the wings?" I had noticed the wrinkles in the skin on the wing-roots. It wasn't surprising considering the velocity of that dive and the terrific strain on pulling out.

"Yeah, but it still flies all right. You take Wehrmann's kite".

"My God!" he said, shaking his head. "I'll see you back at the Mess, if you make it - I want to buy you a drink. After all, you saved my ass!"

"Everyone's entitled to one mistake!" I said.

I was brought back to reality by the pilot's voice.

"You sure seem interested in our route, Colonel. Is this the first time you've flown this route?"

"No - but it's the first time I've been able to admire the scenery!"

"Manston here is a real good airfield with a nice, clear approach to the main runway."

"So I've heard!" I said.

***

When the Battle of Britain was over, it was exciting that we could afford to carry the war to the enemy; it was a thrill to skim over the Channel and look down on the city of Paris. It was also exciting when we got our P-51 Mustangs and could escort the bombers and look down on Berlin.

But this was something else! We were letting down into Mitchell Field. In the distance, I could see the skyline of New York where I had been born, and below were the distinctive houses of Long Island. I was coming home after four years of combat and a year as a prisoner-of-war.

"Do you want to take her in, Colonel?"

I smiled at the pilot and shook my head.

"The way those controllers have been dictating your every move, a fighter pilot's approach with this big crate would give them a heart-attack - and me a court-martial!"

"I doubt that! There's a reception committee down there loaded with brass!"

The "brass" included Generals Bill Kepner and Tooey Spaatz. I was surprised to see them there. I shouldn't have been; in the 8th Air Force, we'd been lucky with our generals.

"Welcome home, Colonel!"

"Thank you, sir!"

"We'll see you in the Officers' Mess this evening!"

The reception party dispersed and climbed into their jeeps and staff cars. Two civilians in trench coats who had been hovering in the background came up to me. Behind them were two Military Police. I'm six feet tall, but I had to look up at their expressionless faces.

"Colonel Goodson, unfortunately we have to ask you to come with us."

"Why?"

"For illegal entry into the United States."

"You're joking, of course!"

"I'm afraid not. In 1940, you joined the RAF and swore allegiance to the King of England."

"But Roosevelt passed an Act of Congress restoring our US nationality!"

"Your case is special. You didn't have five years consecutive residence in the United States. That means that at the age of 21 you had to make a choice; and at the age of 21 you had sworn allegiance to a foreign country and were serving in their armed forces. We believe that constitutes a choice. But please don't worry! We have made arrangements for you to appear in Court this afternoon to be re-naturalised. It will only take an hour."

"I don't believe this! Do you know what these are?" I pointed to my rows of ribbons and the US Air Force wings. "How could I have got those if I was a foreigner?"

"We know those are the highest American decorations and we know what you've done to get them. It's very embarrassing, but they don't affect the question of your nationality!"

"This is ridiculous, and I have no intention of going anywhere with you! I have an appointment with General Spaatz and General Kepner. They know damned well I'm an American!"

The two towering MPs moved closer to me, but so did a figure in RAF uniform who had been listening quietly in the background.

"Actually, they're probably quite right you know, old boy. If I were you, I'd go along with them. It'll be quicker and simpler than fighting the red tape!"

"Who are you?"

"Group-Captain Donaldson, British Air Attaché in Washington."

He wore only two ribbons, but one was the Distinguished Service Order and the other was the Distinguished Flying Cross with Bar. Now I recalled the name.

"Are you the Donaldson who was with 601 Squadron at Tangmere in '40?"

"Yes - were you there then?"

"I was a lowly Sergeant-Pilot in 43 Squadron, but we all knew you by reputation. I once flew as tail-end Charlie when you were leading the Wing! Now, you tell these idiots they're out of their minds!"

He looked at me calmly. "Did you trust me when I led the Tangmere Wing?"

"Of course!"

"Then trust me now!"

I allowed myself to be guided into a car by the two Immigration Officials and driven to a courthouse in Jamaica. The place was jammed with immigrants. It took my mind back to Europe and the hordes of refugees flooding westwards ahead of the Russians.

There were bearded peasants and their families, the women wearing shawls over their heads; there were Hasidic Jews with their big black hats and side curls; there were Arabs, Orientals, Hispanics; every race, nationality and colour was there, all becoming instant Americans.

The two officials escorted me through and we were soon standing in front of the Court. The proceedings started immediately with the arrival of the Judge.

He was obviously bored with these duties, which he probably conducted every day, and he was anxious to get them over with as soon as possible. He rattled off his speech in a strong Brooklyn-Jewish accent, which even I could hardly understand, and only looked up when he got to:

"Raise-ya-right-hands-de-ya-swear-never-to-bear-arms-against-da-govvamant-o-da-Unided-States..."

At this point, his eye fell on me.

This was not surprising. A tall officer in full uniform with three rows of ribbons, RAF and USAF wings, standing at the front of that rather nondescript crowd could hardly be inconspicuous. Almost without pausing in his rapid-fire recitiation, he said with a mixture of incredulity, annoyance and resignation:

"What the hell are you doing here?"

One of the officials rushed up to him with a file of papers and started to explain. The Judge raised his eyes to Heaven, raised his hands palms upwards, in an eloquent gesture which said more plainly than words "This should happen to me!"

After swearing to defend the Flag and refrain from overthrowing the United States Government, I became the second Colonel in the US Army to become an American citizen. The first was George

Washington.

In the Officers' Mess that evening, Donaldson came up to me at the bar.

"You owe me a drink, I think," he said pleasantly. "It's Scotch and a dash of soda, no ice!"

"Be my guest - but I didn't think you were very helpful today!"

"Not today, but tomorrow!" he said.

"Why? What happens tomorrow?"

"You'll pick up your back pay. All the time you've been in prison camp, your pay has been mounting up. You should get about $8000, but make sure they don't deduct US Income Tax."

"What do you mean?"

"The Internal Revenue Service takes the attitude that US citizens pay tax wherever they may be resident, even in a German PoW camp. His Majesty's Government, on the other hand, would consider taxing a PoW as adding insult to injury; so you see, you owe me and your immigration officials a debt of gratitude!"

I started to laugh, and then started to think.

"You know, there's one thing I can't understand. Who would have informed the US Immigration authorities that I had sworn allegiance to the King?"

"Can't imagine, old boy! Cheers!"

He raised his glass to me, knocked back his whisky with obvious relish and turned to the barman.

"Same again, please. No ice!"

***

For most fighting men coming home, the words "Returning Hero" have a hollow ring, but not for those returning to New York in 1945. It wasn't just the official receptions, the ticker-tape parades, the public appearances and the press conferences; it was the people.

They cheered us, they screamed at us, they waved to us, they laughed at us, they cried for us; they wanted to touch us, they wanted to buy us drinks, they wanted us to know they were grateful and that they loved us.

The others took it for granted, but my old friend Millie was concerned. It was his serious approach to everything he undertook that made Millard Milliken the most reliable man in my squadron, with his fifteen victories all ones he had picked off as they were about to shoot down one of our planes.

"Do you think they mean it?" he asked me as we got back to our hotel.

"That's the trouble - they're absolutely sincere. So be careful! If it keeps up, even you will start believing you're a hero!"

"No, not me, and not you. We've been in prison camp, remember? We've had all that stuff knocked out of us!"

"Still, it's nice". I paused. "Except..."

"Except what?"

"Except for those who aren't around to enjoy it."

"They wouldn't mind. We all ran the same risks. We were just the lucky ones."

"I'm thinking more about the next of kin. How do you think they feel about all this? Everyone going crazy with joy, a bunch of stuck-up, over-decorated fighter pilots strutting in front of the cameras, and all they've got is their broken hearts - and no-one giving a damn!"

"Maybe they don't feel that way."

"Well, maybe we'll find out. I've got to call one of them."

"Who's that?"

"Pete Lehman's father."

"Why call him?"

"Pete asked me to."

"You mean he knew he wasn't going to make it?"

"I guess he figured that was a pretty strong possibility. That's why he was so keen to get a Distinguished Flying Cross. When I told him he had been recommended for it, he kept asking when it would come through. I asked him why it was so important to him. He didn't answer for a few seconds, and when he did, he was more serious than I had ever seen him.

"First," he said, "because I'm Jewish and I want to show we can fight, but second and more important, I'm adopted. My father is the greatest man I know and I want the DFC as a present for his 70th birthday to show him I didn't let him down."

"Did he make it?" asked Millie.

"Only just. We got the citation dated on the old man's birthday alright. It was the 28th of March, 1944. Pete was killed on March 31st."

"Are you going to see the old man?"

"Hell, no! I doubt if I'll even get through to him on the 'phone. You know who he is?"

Millie shook his head.

"He's head of Lehman Brothers, one of the leading investment banking firms in the world, and is now Governor of the State of New York. I've got a 'phone number here. I'll just leave a message that I called."

The secretary was cool and efficient and asked where she could contact me. I figured that was that, and went out to drink in the sights of the city where I was born and which I hadn't seen for over six years.

I walked up Fifth Avenue to the Park, had a drink in the Plaza and thought back to the prison camp and the misery of Europe, another world, another century ago.

When I got back to the hotel and picked up my room key, the clerk said, "There's a gentleman been waiting to see you."

He nodded to a short, elderly, thickset man, who came towards me.

"Colonel," he said, "I came straight over when I got your message. I hope you'll excuse me, but I wanted to say 'Welcome Home' and thank you for what you did for us. Peter Lehman was my son and he always spoke so highly of you."

"I'm privileged to have flown with him. He was a fine man. You should be very proud of him."

"I am! He got the DFC, you know!"

"Yes, I know. It was his birthday present for you."

I looked into his eyes and saw that they had lost their bright glint and were clouded over with sorrow, and when he spoke his voice had lost it's efficient crispness and became choked with pain. He was no longer the Governor of New York, nor even the powerful international banker.

"Yes, I know, he was a good boy," whispered Pete's Dad.

***

This was more like it - a chauffeur-driven car, a nice new uniform, and a few rows of pretty medal ribbons on my chest; quite a change from a shabby khaki shirt and slacks and Stalag-Luft III!

We were gliding through the neat and leafy old residential section of Dayton, Ohio, on our way to the USAAF base at Wright Field, where I was preparing to take a jet squadron to the Far East.

"Tell me, driver, who lives in these beautiful old wooden houses?"

"I don't really know, sir, but I guess some of the old Dayton families. That one there is the old Wright residence. They say Orville Wright still lives there."

I was surprised. "Surely the Wright Brothers died years ago?"

"No, Wilbur died a while back, but I think Orville is still alive."

"Stop the car!"

I walked up to the door and rang the bell. The door was opened by a small, bald man.

"Mr Wright?"

"Yup, I'm Orville Wright."

He spoke with an old Ohio accent and his voice and his smile were friendly and welcoming. I apologised for disturbing him, explained who I was and added that it was an unexpected pleasure and honour to be able to speak with the first man to fly.

"Shucks!" he said. "It's a pleasure for me to talk to a flyer! I'd like to hear about your experiences - come on in!"

"Well, they're waiting for me out at the base, but I'd love to come by this evening if that wouldn't be too inconvenient."

"Any time!"

That evening was the first of many pleasant chats. He talked easily and modestly about the early days when he and Wilbur worked in their bicycle shop on the first airframes and of their many frustrations. Any engine with enough power to lift the plane in theory was so heavy it defeated its own purpose. This was one reason they went down to Kittyhawk on the coast of Carolina, where the almost constant winds coming off the Atlantic and up the dunes gave them extra lift.

He showed me letters they had received from aviation pioneers in Europe: Forman in France, Daimler in Germany, Sopwith in England, Fokker in Holland. Much of this correspondence was concerned with the problem of torque, whereby the rapid rotation of the propeller induced a dangerous roll of the aircraft in the opposite direction. The faster the propeller rotated, the more the aircraft tended to roll in the opposite direction, so that the more the engine power was improved, the stronger became the torque factor, until the pilot wouldn't have the strength to correct with his controls and the plane would roll into the ground.

Many of the letters they received were full of algebraic equations, which Orville happily admitted were all Greek to him and Wilbur. It was the Wright brothers' common-sense approach which eventually solved the problem.

"Wilbur grabbed one wing tip and twisted in one direction, and I got ahold of the other wing-tip and twisted it in the opposite direction. It wasn't very scientific, I guess, but it worked!"

He showed the same attitude to high-technology when I took him out to Wright Field and sat him in the cockpit of the latest jet fighter. He listened patiently as we explained the controls and the mass of complicated instruments. When we had finished, he looked at us quizzically with a twinkle in his eye.

"You reckon it'll fly?"

"Yessir! Faster than the speed of sound!"

"Yeah, that's a lot faster than our old Flyer - but not as much fun!"

We looked down at him, looking so small in the cockpit, and saw a smile on his lips and a far-away look in his eyes. He may have been mesmerised by the array of modern techonology in front of him, but I suspect he was back in that other plane, exposed to the wind, wrestling that contraption of wire, struts and fabric into the air at Kittyhawk, the day man flew for the first time. I helped him out of the cockpit.

"No sir! It's not as much fun!"

One day, I had a 'phone call from Eddie Rickenbacker, America's leading Ace in WWI and at that time, President of Eastern Airlines.

"Jim," he said, "we're having our annual dinner in a couple of months and, as you know, we always try to get an outstanding speaker. The Committee has unanimously agreed that you would be ideal. Will you accept?"

"You can do better than that, Eddie. There are lots of more impressive speakers than me you could get."

"Name one!"

After a few suggestions which were turned down, I had a brain-wave.

"What about Orville Wright?"

"Yeah! Very funny!"

"I'm serious. He'd be great."

"You mean he's still around?"

"Alive and well and living right here in Dayton!"

Of course, Eddie was delighted, but he left it to me to persuade Orville to do it.

"Shucks! I can't speak in public! Anyway, no-one will want to listen to an old goat like me. Most people think I'm dead, anyway, so let's leave it that way!"

"But Mr. Wright, this is a small gathering of great aviators, many of whom you've known, and all of whom think you are the greatest man in the history of aviation! You wouldn't even have to do a thing except stand up and say "Hello" to them, and you'd give them the thrill of their lives!"

I reeled off some of the great names that were expected to be there.

"Yes," he said, "I know Eddie Rickenbacker, and I remember Lindberg and Jimmy Doolittle and Hap Arnold and Rosendahl and Harry Bruno and - yeah, I guess you're right, I'll see a lot of old friends. O.K., I'll go."

On the night of the dinner, I gazed around the large hall. They were packed in shoulder to shoulder.

"I thought you said this was going to be a small gathering!" said Orville.

Eddie Rickenbacker came to my rescue.

"Well, usually it is, but when they heard you were going to be here, they came from all over the country. We've had to turn a lot of people away."

As he led Orville to the top table, the crowd rose to give him a standing ovation which lasted for a full two minutes.

Eddie Rickenbacker was always a dramatic character and an eloquent speaker, but when he introduced his guest that evening, he excelled himself. As far as I can remember, it went something like this:

"We have just won the greatest and most terrible war in the history of mankind; a war in which almost every nation and every individual was directly or indirectly involved. The most important factor in our victory was air power. Vast fleets of bombers, protected by swarms of fighters, reduced our enemies' cities to ruins, annihilated their war potential, sank their navies and immobilised their armies.

"We now stand on the threshold of a new era in which fleets of great planes will carry millions of people to the furthest corners of the globe in less time than it took our grandparents to travel to Albany, the State capital. Thanks to aviation, we can now look forward to a future of international understanding with peace and prosperity.

"Yet fifty years ago, no-one would have dreamed of what today we take for granted. Two men had the dream and the courage and genius to make that dream came true.

"Gentlemen, it is my privilege and honour to be able to introduce one of them, the great pioneer of aviation, the first man to fly, Mr. Orville Wright!"

When the ovation finally died down, Orville looked impishly around the assembly and said, "My name is Orville Wright."

Another round of spontaneous applause.

"And that's about the only thing in that wonderful introduction by my friend Eddie that bears any relation to the truth! I'm sorry, Eddie, I guess I should just accept your praise and bask in glory, but I'm afraid I'm too honest. If you had come by our bicycle shop in Dayton and told me there'd be fleets of airplanes destroying whole cities and flying thousands of people all round the world, we'd have told you you were plumb crazy. We had no such vision. We were just a couple of kids, trying to get a clumsy, underpowered contraption into the air - and, more important, to get it down again in one piece!"

His smiling face clouded.

"In fact, we once decided to give it all up. When the Army asked us to train Lieutenant Selfridge as a pilot, we fitted a second seat in front of the pilot's seat. I took off with my friend Selfridge, I couldn't control the plane, and we crashed. Lt. Selfridge was killed.

"I said to Wilbur, 'That proves that an aircraft can never carry more than one person.' Wilbur agreed. 'It just isn't worth it - we'll call it all off'.

"It was the Army that persuaded us to go on, because they saw the potential of the airplane in war. If it wasn't for them, we'd have stopped right there - and someone else would have been the first to fly!"

The dinner was a great success and Orville enjoyed it as much as anyone.

The next day when we flew back to Dayton, the airline hostess came over as we landed and asked Orville if he had had a good flight.

"Yup," he said. "I've had a good flight."

"Was it your first flight?"

"No," he said, "but that was a good flight, too!"

He looked up at me and winked.

*****

Chapter 8

SENTIMENTAL JOURNEY

The General folded the 201 file and looked at me.

"That's just about the most impressive record I've ever read. Are you sure we can't persuade you to stay on? The Air Force needs officers like you and, with a background like that, you could end up right at the top. Think it over, Colonel!"

"Thanks, General, but I've thought it over. I have the offer of a job in business and I think I'd better start working for a living as soon as possible."

"There's plenty of work in the Air Force! Now that the war's over, we've got an enormous job of re-organising and making sure we stay strong enough to preserve the peace. We don't want any more Pearl Harbours!"

"I can't imagine that happening, sir, but if it does, you have my address."

"O.K. You've got a lot of back leave due to you. Why don't you take it and see how you feel afterwards?"

"I don't really need a rest, sir." I paused.

"Well, what is it?"

"Well, I suppose it's foolish, but now that it's all over I'm thinking of those good friends who weren't so lucky as me, and I feel guilty. During the war when I wrote letters of condolence, I often rashly promised the next of kin that I'd visit them after the war. It was foolish of me, but at that time the end of the war seemed very remote, and my chances of seeing it remoter still. Now, those promises are pricking my conscience."

"I think that's a great idea! Why don't you go see them?"

"But how? Some of them are from my RAF days and came from places as far away as New Zealand!"

"No problem - you can use MATS. You'd have to wait around for space on a 'plane, but you'd get there eventually. Our Military Air Transport Service covers the whole world."

I was no longer so sure it was a good idea, but before I knew it my orders were cut and I found myself in a military transport, droning on over the seemingly endless expanse of the Pacific. What the hell was I doing going half-way round the world to see people I didn't know and with whom I would have nothing in common? And what on earth could I say to such people?

I wished I hadn't started with the most difficult and most remote. But it was inevitable that New Zealand would be on my list. Although there was no conscription, almost every able-bodied man volunteered, so the number of New Zealanders in the RAF was out of all proportion to the small home population of 3 million.

John Kempton-Werohiea had been not only a New Zealander, but a Maori. To me, he was my friend when I needed one.

It was early in the war, when things looked blackest. We were based at Kenley, south of Croydon. As we were bombed and strafed, we moved from one to another of Kenley's satellites, including Redhill. It was lovely countryside and there was always a good pub not far away. As we walked down to the pub on those glorious summer evenings, we gazed at the green of the hedgrows and fields and breathed in the smell of hawthorn or new-mown hay and it was like the breath of life.

We needed a breath of life. We had too much death. Death in the air was one thing, but at least it was clean; a few seconds of screaming radio chatter whilst your're racking your own plane around in a tight break, sweating, swearing and praying. Sometimes there was a funeral to attend in the local church, but the very antiquity of the scene helped to put death in perspective.

It was the ground attacks that hurt most; burning planes, destroyed as they tried to take off, becoming funeral pyres for young pilots; the bodies of ground personnel, including the girls of the WAAF, lying like broken dolls where they were gunned down by strafing Me-109s. That's when it really came home and you felt the need to get away from it.

The pubs did help, but they became almost like officers' or sergeants' Messes; the same anxious young faces, the same brave talk of "good shows", the same brave jokes and pretence of "couldn't care less".

That's why you had to get away to London once in a while.

Getting there wasn't too difficult. Getting back in time to stand dawn readiness was another thing, as the trains didn't run at night. That's where Stripey came in.

It was John Kempton-Werohiea who master-minded the deal. None of us paid much attention when we read in the local newspaper that a small travelling circus had to close down and sell its animals because of the war and shortages. John alone had the foresight to see that this could provide the solution to our transport problems.

We didn't catch on when John drove past the open-mouthed guards at the gate in a small vehicle called a trap, pulled by a zebra. We just thought he'd gone round the bend. He had to explain.

"The circus couldn't feed him, so I got him and the trap for seven pounds. We've got a whole airfield of grass and we can even cadge grain from the local farmers. In return, we've got transport to London and back!"

The next evening, with Ray Fusch from St. Louis, Phil Gofton from Medicine Hat, Manitoba, and with John driving, we trotted through Croydon on the A23 to London behind Stripey, the zebra. John was big and heavy and none of us were small, but little Stripey was game and strong and the road was smooth and almost deserted.

In a couple of hours, we arrived in Hyde Park, where we took Stripey out of the shafts, put a rather large halter on him, tethered him to a tree and caught the Tube from Hyde Park Corner to Piccadilly Circus and the Crackers Club.

Sometime around midnight, we strolled back to the tree where we had left Stripey, to find an empty halter lying on the grass - and no Stripey. John seemed to have some experience of horses if not zebras, and was unperturbed.

"He can't have gone far. He's probably looking for a place that has more grass, so let's look for him over there, where it's more open."

The four of us took off and were stumbling through the dark calling "Stripey! Stripey!" when we were confronted by a London bobby. He was very polite.

"Now gentlemen, isn't it time to call it a day and go home?"

"Yes, of course, constable," said John, equally politely. "We're just looking for our zebra - he must be around here somewhere!"

"Now, now, sir! I think you should all go home and get some sleep and you'll feel much better in the morning!"

"But you don't understand! We want to go home. We have to stand dawn readiness. But we can't go home until we find our zebra. Please help us to find him - he's easy to spot, he's got black and white stripes. It'll only take a few minutes to find him!"

"Alright, sir, I'll give you five minutes, if you agree to go home then."

"Fine! We'll spread out a bit and start off in this direction. If anyone spots him, give a shout!"

We hadn't gone far before we heard a startled shout. Turning in that direction, we found the policeman standing stockstill, mouth wide open, staring in absolute disbelief at our zebra.

John came up with the halter and the nosebag of oats and we were soon leading Stripey back to his trap. The bobby was still standing there and his mouth was still open.

***

We were all on dawn readiness, that is, all of us that were left. The squadron should have had twelve flying, with six reserves. We had only ten flying, with no reserves. What was worse, Wing had told us we were to send two of them down to Lympne.

The forward airfields, like Hawkinge behind Folkestone and Manston near Ramsgate were under constant attack by the Luftwaffe, so we'd learned the hard way that we couldn't leave planes down there overnight. Every morning, two planes would take off from the main airfields of Kenley, Biggin Hill, West Malling or Gravesend, land at the forward bases and, without getting out of their planes, the pilots would wait to be scrambled when the enemy planes came over.

It was a lousy job and we all hated it. The 109s could come in low over the coast so that the radar didn't pick them up; that meant they often shot up our planes before we could get off the ground. Even if we did get off, two of us would find ourselves up against hordes of

109s.

"Woody, it's about your turn for Hawkinge. Goodson's your wingman. Here's the line-up for the rest of you."

That's about all the briefing the C.O. ever gave us in those days. It was all he needed to give - we all knew the score.

John came up to me as we walked out of the briefing.

"Bad luck, Goody! I really wish I could do it for you!"

"I know - thanks!"

Woodward and the C.O. were just ahead of us. The "old man" - who must have been all of 25 - shrugged in apology. Woody nodded and slapped him on the shoulder. They said it better than we did, but then they'd been together longer.

Woody and I circled over Folkestone, landed on the grass of Hawkinge, taxied back, turned into wind and shut off our engines. From somewhere, a petrol bowser appeared and a young woman in WAAF uniform topped up our tanks. Two batteries were wheeled up and plugged into our Hurricanes so that we could start the engines as soon as the red flare came curling up from the little hut where the corporal sat, waiting for the telephone to ring.

We greatly admired the ground crews at those forward bases. They were almost constantly under fire. I always felt like a traitor in the evening when we took off for the relative peace of our home base, leaving them behind.

Meanwhile, we sat in our cockpits and silently prayed that there would be no red flares; for a few hours, the prayers even seemed to be working. The wind was from the northeast, so we were parked on the southeast side of the small, grassy field. Behind us was a valley, and behind that, Folkestone and the Channel. We frequently craned round to check that no-one was paying us a surprise visit.

Suddenly, when we least expected it, the window of the hut opened and the red flare arced out. We pushed the buttons, the props turned slowly and the engines coughed into life. The propellers started to spin, we opened the throttles fully and were bumping over the grass, my plane about twenty yards to the right of Woody's and ten yards behind.

Just before my tail came up, I found myself staring fascinatedly at a trail of dust-spurts snaking after Woody's plane. Everything seemed to be happening in slow motion. The snake caught up with him, and the plane exploded in a burst of flame.

I braked and stomped on left rudder. As my plane screamed into a ground loop, a second snake went past me. It passed where my plane would have been a second later. The left undercarriage collapsed and the Hurricane slewed to a stop in a cloud of dust. My head went forward and hit the instrument panel.

When my head cleared, I undid my Sutton harness and parachute and clambered out of the open cockpit. I tried to run to Woody's plane. It was too late. It was a flaming wreck. The crash wagon drew up, strong hands grabbed me and pulled me away.

In the Sergeants' Mess that evening I was sitting alone. The others had sensed I didn't want company. Only one knew I needed him. John Kempton-Werohiea lumbered up and slumped down beside me. For five minutes neither of us spoke, then John said one word.

"Baa-stards!"

I was surprised, because he was usually so easy-going.

"I guess they were just doing their job, like us."

"I don't mean the bloody Krauts! I mean those bloody politicians who allowed the damn pacifists to starve the armed services of guns and planes, so that poor sods like you and Woody and I have to go up day after day against hopeless odds!"

"Well, if it's any consolation, we've learned our lesson. It could never happen again."

"I just hope that consoles Woody and his next of kin!"

Back at the dispersal hut, I saw John arguing with Mac. Mac was a flight-lieutenant from Toronto who'd been around long enough to acquire a DFC and a "couldn't care less" attitude. I saw Mac shrug and John turned away and ran into the hut.

I was standing on the wing about to flop my parachute into the cockpit when I saw the great bulk of John Kempton-Weohiea lumbering up.

"Get down! I'm taking your place!"

"The hell you are! I'm flying No. 2 to Mac!"

"It's O.K. with Mac - I talked to him."

"Forget it, John! I'm O.K. and I'm going to fly!"

The next thing I knew, John had lurched up on the wing and I was sliding down it. I landed on my back on the ground. Before I could pick up myself and my 'chute, John was in the cockpit. The engine started and the Hurricane rolled forward, leaving me in the blast from the prop.

The Squadron was scrambled twice during the day. As often happened, there were a few skirmishes, but no claims and no losses, though everyone was kept busy enough not to worry about the two planes down at Lympne. It was not until it got dark and they were not back that I went to find the Intelligence Officer. He'd just got the news.

"Mac and Werohiea were bounced on take-off by a gaggle of Me-109s. Mac crashed before he got his wings up. John apparently managed to get airborne, but they lost radio contact with him. The Observer Corps at Hythe reported a dog-fight off the coast and a 109 and a Hurricane crashing into the sea."

It was some time before I learned more. It came from an "official source".

It was in the Salted Almond Bar of the Trocadero in Shaftesbury Avenue. I was sitting opposite a good-looking girl in a WAAF uniform and my intentions were not honourable. It was not her beauty that interested me, however, nor her brains; it was the fact that she was one of those brave young girls who pushed little arrows around a vast map with long rakes; who had to control their emotions as they listened to the prayers, curses and screams of the pilots thousands of feet above them.

She didn't want to talk about it.

"He was a New Zealander, wasn't he?"

"Yes," I said.

"Well, it isn't true that we lost RT contact with him. We ordered him to return to base, but he just kept asking for a vector onto the German fighters. Finally, he said, 'Tally-ho! and thanks!'"

"And that was all?"

"No, not quite. We heard one more word."

"What was that?"

"It was a swear word." I waited for it. "It was Bastards!"

"Thanks!" I said.

***

That was when I made the promise which led to my being in a transport plane heading for Rotorua and wondering more and more how I had ever been fool enough to embark on this useless adventure.

In the first place, the promise had been made only to myself, so no-one would have been any the wiser if I had reneged. What's more, I had only known John for a few weeks and I knew nothing at all about his family. In fact, I had addressed my letter to them simply to Rotorua, assuming that there couldn't be many Kempton-Werohieas in what I presumed was the small town of Rotorua.

No answer had come by the time I took off. Perhaps he had no living relatives. Maybe, even if he did, I wouldn't be able to find them; I had already learned that Rotorua was a lot bigger than I had thought. Even if I found them what could I say to them?

I imagined myself in a mud hut, trying to speak pidgin English with a large family of Maoris who couldn't understand who I was or what in the world I was doing there. I would have turned back if I could, but the plane droned on until the pilot announced he was letting down into the airport.

We landed and started to taxi towards the control tower. When we stopped, the pilot came back and said, "They've directed us to the northeast corner and hold."

When we got there I saw a cavalcade of cars heading towards us. The lead car was a Rolls-Royce with two flags on the front. As it pulled up to the plane, an aide-de-camp in full uniform and gold braid got out and stood to attention. I was asked to go down the steps. I returned the officer's salute, wondering what was going on. The aide explained.

"His Excellency the Governor has expressed the wish that you accept his invitation to meet him at Government House."

I was ushered into the Rolls and whisked away. I eventually found myself approaching an imposing building, at the door of which stood a dignified giant of a gentleman in full uniform, who greeted me warmly.

"How wonderful of you to come, Colonel! Thank you, thank you! We have taken the liberty of preparing a room for you!"

"Your Excellency, I'm deeply honoured, but I feel there's been some mistake. I just came here to visit the family of a war-time friend of mine, John Kempton-Werohiea."

"Didn't they tell you? John was my son!"

I didn't know what to say, or what to do. The Governor knew that. He stepped forward and embraced me.

"God bless you, my son!" he whispered.

*****

Chapter 9

TEARS ON A ROW OF MEDAL RIBBONS

Richmond, Virginia, is a fine city with a great many beautiful residences and a prosperous business centre.

But that wasn't where we were now. The command car the base commander had lent to me was lurching wildly into one muddy pothole after another. The shabby old clapboard buildings were falling apart and the area in front of them looked like a rubbish dump. The few parked cars were stripped, rusty wrecks, sitting sadly on their brake-drums. Not only their tyres but their wheels had gone.

On the broken wooden porches, those who lived in this black slum slept, drank beer out of cans, or stared blankly at the Air Force car with its smart Air Force driver and the uniformed, highly-decorated officer in the back.

"Sir, this can't be right - you must have the wrong address!"

"Keep going, Corporal, we're not going to give up now."

"This guy must have meant a lot to you, sir."

"Not really," I said. "I only knew him for a couple of days."

"I guess I can't understand. See, I just missed the war, dammit! I just can't imagine what war is like. Maybe you can explain, sir. I'd really appreciate it!"

I looked at the young corporal, shook my head and said to myself, "No, son, I can't explain. All I can do is remember."

I closed my eyes and I was back in the Ops. Room of 8th Air Force Fighter Command in early 1944, where the chain of events started which had led me to Richmond two years later. There were two Generals and my Base Commander, Don Blakeslee in the room and I was arguing with General Bill Kepner.

"But sir, I can't take my Squadron away now! You yourself said the present bombing programme will build up until D-Day, by which time the Luftwaffe Fighter Command has to be hit badly enough to be knocked out as a factor in stopping the invasion! Besides, our Group is the most experienced in long-range escort and the bombers are still taking a hell of a beating over the target out there!"

"Major, we're not sending your Squadron to the Fifteenth - just you. Believe me, your mission down there will be just as full of action as anything you'd get here, and a damn sight more important!"

I didn't argue any more. Bill Kepner knew what he was doing and he'd never sold any of us down the river. Besides, he was a General, and there was another General there. I wasn't going to argue with him, either. After all, they had asked Jimmy Doolittle to fly to Tokyo when there was no way of flying back!

"When do I start, sir?"

"Tomorrow!"

I saluted and turned to leave.

"Oh, and Major..."

"Sir?"

"You have my word - we won't start the invasion without you!"

I had talked them into letting me take my own plane. They expected me to follow the route used by the transport planes, over Cornwall and Gibraltar. I had pointed out that a Mustang with droppable tanks had the range to fly directly over Europe to North Africa. Even if German fighters took off to intercept, they could hardly get up to 30,000ft. in time to catch it. My orders gave me emergency priority, so they gave me clearance with some obvious misgivings.

I shared those misgivings as I fought my way up through 30,000ft. of cloud and turbulence. I was comforted by the thought that German fighter pilots were not good at instrument flying and probably wouldn't even take off; but that wouldn't help me to find my way to North Africa if the cloud didn't clear.

I was still flying blind when the fuel in the drop tanks ran out. I switched to the internal tanks, thanked the Lord when the engine picked up again, and jettisoned the drop tanks. I thought of some French farmer finding them in a field and wondering where they came from! I trimmed the plane and felt very naked, miles up with no extra fuel.

Just when I felt I couldn't watch those little dials and fight the turbulence any longer, I felt snatches of sunlight breaking through. I'd been on instruments for about four hours, but now I could see the ground. On the left were the Alps and far ahead I could see what had to be the Mediterranean. The map of Southern Europe was stretched out before me. Once more, I was lord of all I surveyed. Way down there was worry and war. It was better up here!

I flew over the Mediterranean, past Corsica and Sardinia in a shallow dive and, much sooner than I expected, I was over North Africa. I was heading for a US air base, but when I raised them on the radio, they diverted me to an RAF base well to the east "for operational reasons". That meant they had planes returning from a mission.

The alternative base was small and hard to find, but soon I was coming in to a yellow-brown dirt runway. When I pulled up in front of the control tower and pulled off my helmet, an RAF man who had been waving me in climbed up on my wing.

"Where have you flown in from, sir?"

"Manston, in Kent."

He looked at me in amazement. "When did you take off?"

"About seven hours ago."

"You mean you were in England this morning?"

"That's right".

The look in his eyes changed from amazement to wistfulness.

"Tell me, sir, is it still as green as ever?"

I looked around at the sand and dirt and the shabby tents and huts and knew that, for all the months and years this Englishman had been in this arid, alien land, pushed from one miserable airfield to another, he had dreamed of the greenness of England, so far away in another world. He wanted an answer, he needed reassurance.

"Yes," I said, "it's still as green as ever!"

My interview with General Bourne of the Fifteenth Air Force was a classic of economy with words.

"We have to have more long-range fighter escorts for our bombers. We've just got deliveries of P-51 Mustangs and we've got a Fighter Group based in Corsica. Trouble is, they've been flying P-39 Air-cobras. Your job is to get them operational on P-51s immediately. Any questions?"

"Yes sir. Who is the Commanding Officer there?"

"For the time being, you are!"

Thinking of the coming air offensive out of England leading up to the invasion, I asked, "How long do you think the assignment will take?"

"That's up to you!"

I flew out over the Mediterranean again. I had filed a flight plan, but no-one had seemed very interested in it. After the highly-organised operations of the 8th Air Force in England, this theatre seemed somehow less professional and lacking in enthusiasm.

I veered towards the Italian mainland and from 25,000ft. peered down at Salerno and Anzio, where the Allies were pinned down. Then I tried to raise the radio tower at Chisoni, without much luck. I figured they must have set my radio to the wrong wave-length. Anyway, I had a map on which the new airfields had been marked. The weather was good and the eastern side of Corsica not so large that I couldn't identify the airfield with the P-51s dispersed around it.

As I landed and taxied to the control-tower, I saw a few figures running towards it. I parked the plane in front of the tower, a jeep raced up and two MPs jumped out. They stared at my name and rank on the plane and the neat little rows of swastikas. I slipped out of my harness and helmet, fished my peaked cap from under the seat, clapped it on my head, climbed out of the cockpit and slid down the wing root to the ground. The two MPs saluted.

"There's a kitbag jammed in the cockpit. I'll check in with the control tower, then you can take me to the Officers' Mess."

They were still at the salute as I strode towards the tower. Inside was a startled corporal.

"Your radio working, corporal?"

"Yessir!"

"Why couldn't I contact you?"

"I dunno, sir."

"Were you expecting me?"

"No, sir."

"Was this post manned?"

"I dunno, sir."

I was getting annoyed, but I controlled my temper, sensing that something was drastically wrong. I pointed to the 'phone.

"Get me the Acting Commanding Officer!"

"Yessir! Who would that be, sir?"

"There has to be someone in command, even if it's a sergeant! Who is it?"

"Dunno, sir."

I grabbed the 'phone. A bored voice at the other end said "Yeah?"

"Major Goodson here. Give me the Duty Officer!"

"Duty Officer? Who's that?"

"Sir!"

"What?"

"Sir!" I shouted.

Something clicked. The tone changed. "Yes, sir!"

"If there's no Duty Officer, get me the Admin. Officer!"

"Yessir!"

After a few minutes, I had a nervous Admin. Officer on the line. We agreed to meet in the Officers' Mess. I went down to my plane where the MPs were waiting by the jeep.

"Officers' Mess!" I said.

"Yessir!" said the sergeant, and we took off.

"Where's your officer, Sergeant?" I asked.

"In Calvi."

"What's he doing in Calvi?"

"Trying to round up the flying officers, sir."

"What are the flying officers doing in Calvi?"

"Most of them went over the hill, sir."

"Why?"

"They don't like the new P-51s, sir."

"Can you contact the pilots?"

"Most of them, sir. Calvi's not all that big."

The Officers' Mess was a prefabricated hut, like most of the accomodation on the base. We marched in and found it empty except for four nervous officers: The Admin. Officer, an Engineering Officer, a Medical Officer and a Chaplain.

From them, the story gradually emerged. When the Group arrived to join the 15th Air Force, their morale was good and, like all pilots, they had confidence in the plane they were flying. Unfortunately, their planes were P-39 Aircobras. It soon became obvious that the Allison engine didn't give the plane either the speed, range or altitude to compete and they were therefore replaced by Mustangs.

They should have been delighted to get the best Allied fighter there was, but the planes were not accompanied by any instructors to check the pilots out on them, or at least to warn them of the dangerous differences between the long-range Mustangs and the little Aircobras. In fact, many of the most experienced officers and commanders got transfers to other units.

Their biggest problem was learning to take off with full internal tanks and two 108 gallon external tanks slung beneath the wings. With that load, you had to forget you were flying a fighter, use a lot more runway, not lift off until the airspeed was well above normal take-off speed, and always keep the plane as straight as possible to prevent the fuel sloshing around and destabilising the aircraft.

I suppose the ground crews were as unfamiliar with the new aircraft as the pilot. Whatever the reason, I couldn't ask the pilots. The first four to take off in the new aircraft crashed on take-off.

That did it. The weeks of frustration, indecision, failure and shame reached their climax.

The four officers told me their story with scandalised censure of the pilots and prim satisfaction at their own role.

"Major, I want to assure you that, in spite of the disgraceful conduct of the pilots, the administration of the 999th Group is still functioning perfectly!"

I looked sternly at the Admin. Officer.

"The only function of the 999th Group is to protect the bombers of the 15th Air Force who are having the hell knocked out of them. This the 999th has not even started to do. And I'm not sure that the crews of those bombers, or their next of kin, will be much consoled to know that, although there were no planes in the air, the administration was functioning perfectly!"

"Major, I'm only concerned with Administration, not the performance of the Group - and I've only just joined it!"

"Funny," I said. "I'm deeply concerned with the performance of the Group - and I've only just joined it!"

The Chaplain felt that he had to defend his fellow officers and himself.

"Major, we all argued with the pilots and told them that, in our opinion, their attitude amounted to mutiny!"

"They must have had very little respect for you and your opinions, since they ignored both."

I turned to the Engineering Officer. "I want to fly every plane myself, with drop tanks, and fully loaded. Please make sure as many as possible are ready to go in about fifteen minutes. I only want to do a circuit and then land."

"Are you going to land with full wing tanks?"

"Yes - but it's the take-off that interests me. It's possible that one or more of the pilots who crashed may have been switched onto drop tanks for take-off, and at full throttle with the plane bumping and sloshing around, there was a short stoppage in the fuel supply."

I cut his protests short. "I'll see you on the flight-line in a few minutes. Now, where is the nearest 'phone? I want to talk to General Bourne. It won't take long, so please wait till I get back."

Ten minutes later, I was back.

"I've just reported to General Bourne that this unit is operational and have requested that we be included on the first available mission. In the meantime, I will be checking out all aircraft and will be available to check out any pilot who wants additional instruction. Please make sure those orders are posted."

I turned to the MP. "Sergeant, you said you could contact the pilots. Please put them in the picture. Right now, you can drive me over to the flight line. Any questions?"

They were in a state of shock. Finally, the Admin. Officer stammered, "But Major, how many pilots do you think will fly?"

"At least one," I told him. "If the pilots in this outfit don't want to follow me, I'm better off without them."

I got into the front seat of the jeep beside the MP.

"What's your name, sergeant?"

"MacNamara, sir."

"Well, Mac, how do you think we're doing?"

He looked at me seriously, then shook his head.

"My God, you really would fly the mission on your own, wouldn't you?"

"You'd better believe it - and you'd better make the others believe it. Make sure they know they now belong to a fighting unit."

"Yes, sir!"

The Engineering Officer greeted me at the dispersal area.

"We've got the plane ready and the tanks loaded. I guess you'll want to get started after lunch?"

"No, I'll skip lunch. I want to check out as many planes as possible before our first mission."

"But when do you expect us to be put on a mission?"

"I told the General we'd be ready at any time."

"Oh, my God!" he said and rushed back to his jeep.

My flights were short. Take-off, a swing over the other two airfields, then up to the town of Calvi and back to land. I knew that this would give the impression that more than one plane was flying and the pilots would want to know what was up.

And it worked. After about an hour, I noticed little groups of pilots gathering to watch the take-offs and landings. Then, as I was walking from one plane to another with my parachute slung over my shoulder, a deep voice with a Southern accent said:

"Major, lemme give you a hand with that."

I turned and looked into a handsome, black and solemn face. His dark, serious eyes looked back into mine with a mixture of uncertainty, fear, determination and other things I didn't understand. What I did understand was that it had taken a lot of courage for him to leave the little group of jeering pilots and walk the few yards across to me.

"Thanks a lot!" I said warmly.

I gave him the 'chute, went on ahead and clambered up onto the wing to take the 'chute from him. I dropped it in the seat, then turned back to him and said:

"Unless you want to take this one up?"

"I'm not checked out on the P-51."

"Well, come on up here. I'll take you through it. There's nothing to it. This is a beautiful plane!"

I put him in the cockpit and went through the whole take-off and landing procedure with him, calling out the airspeeds and every movement. Then we did the same thing for when the plane was loaded down with drop tanks.

"Now," I said, "my plane is over there behind us. Get yourself a chute and a helmet. Plug in and switch on."

"Am I going to fly it?"

I nodded.

"Alone?"

"No," I said. "I'll be with you. What's your name, Lieutenant?"

"Smith, sir. They call me Smitty."

I took off and climbed up over the base. I pushed the transmit button.

"You receiving me, Smitty?"

"Yessir!"

"O.K. Once more from the top. Just like we've been doing. Take off as if you've got tanks. I'll talk you through it again."

I did, and it was beautiful. Just what the audience needed.

"Perfect!" I said.

"Thanks, Major. Now what?"

"Keep flying and spread the Gospel!"

When I landed and moved over to the next plane, a few pilots were hovering around. I waved them over. I went through the check-out without being asked and without getting any comments or questions. They listened in complete silence. But at least they listened.

And they flew. They didn't talk to me, but they flew!

They flew the next day, too, and the next. But would they fly the next? Because that day we got our mission.

It was a long-range mission, escorting bombers to Weiner Neustadt, the industrial centre south of Vienna. The Luftwaffe would come up to protect that one with everything they had.

The evening before, I announced that briefing would be at the main base at dawn. I had appointed an Acting Commanding Officer for each squadron. They weren't necessarily the most experienced or the most senior in rank. I had their 201 files, which had been well-kept, and the non-flying personnel, both officers and men, were very helpful. The final decision was made after personal interview. I had my misgivings, but I've often noticed that the job makes the man. If he's made of the right stuff, he'll rise to the challenge pretty fast.

The problem was that the most eligible candidates were the chief trouble-makers and leaders of the revolt. Still, I took the risk. In every army, probably since the beginning, commanders have followed the rule: Take the officer who complains the most about the food and make him Mess Officer.

It worked with two of the new squadron commanders, but the third wouldn't play. He played the tough guy. He had the physique and aggression of a heavyweight boxer and his sneering and sarcasm covered everyone from Generals on down. I'll call him Hogan. I soon learned that he called me "that stupid prima donna", a name that seemed to have been taken up, at least by Hogan's following.

When I appointed him acting squadron commander, he said, "Oh no! I'm not doing your dirty work for you! Find another stooge!"

I didn't pick a replacement. I would be leading the Group with that squadron anyway, that is, if there was any Group or squadron to lead.

The evening before the briefing, the other two squadron leaders came to me with long faces to announce that their squadrons wouldn't be flying the mission.

"O.K." I said. "But at least bring them to the briefing. After I've left, you can run a Micky Mouse cartoon!"

The next morning, I walked into a crowded briefing room. As I walked to the raised platform, the noise subsided until there was absolute silence.

I spoke slowly and I didn't need to raise my voice.

"Gentlemen, this is a great day for the 999th Fighter Group! Until now, the 999th has been frustrated, abused and misused. Today, that's all over. Today, we are captains of our fate. After today, we can't blame anyone but ourselves. I've told General Bourne that the 999th is ready to take its place in the forefront of the 15th Air Force, because this is a great day for the 15th Air Force, too.

"An hour ago, in another briefing, General Leon Johnson told his bomber crews that the 999th would be protecting them out over the target. For the first time, they won't have to be sitting ducks for the 190s and 109s as they start their run-up to the target. They won't have to watch helplessly as their buddies get shot to pieces. They might even begin to believe they have a chance of surviving their tour of missions. So they'll be counting on the 999th and we're not going to let them down. Here's how we're going to do it."

I took them over every detail, from take-off to touchdown, covering every eventuality. Finally, I asked if there were any questions. I had expected Hogan's Southern drawl, and I got it.

"What makes you think we're going to fly?"

"I don't give a damn what you do! I thought I made it clear - this is a briefing for the 999th Fighter Group, not for some stupid prima donna! I've told you what the 999th is going to do. If you want to know how many planes will be on the mission, the answer is at least one. But I suggest you have a more important question to answer. Some of us are fighting a war. You'd better decide what YOU'RE doing. Any other questions?"

It was Smitty. "Permission to fly as your wingman, sir!"

That was the position that Hogan had been slotted into.

"Check with your squadron commander," I said. "I'll be pressing the starter button at 07.45. It is now 05.32."

At 07.45 I pressed the tit, the prop turned and the engine sprang into life. I stood up in the open cockpit, looked down the field to the next plane and held my breath. Almost imperceptibly, the blades started to move, then there was a puff of smoke from the exhausts and the prop was spinning. One by one, each engine roared into action. I let out a rebel yell, raised my arm and brought it forward in the best traditions of the U.S. Cavalry. The 999th was charging into combat!

My wingman pulled up beside me and gave a thumbs-up sign. It was Smitty.

As I circled upwards, I swivelled around in the cockpit and saw planes slide into sections, sections move into flights, flights swing into squadrons and finally the whole Group of three squadrons straightened out and started the long climb behind me.

We picked up the bombers just south of Graz in Austria as planned and I took my squadron directly over the bomber stream, leaving the other two squadrons to protect them on either side, as planned. Even the Luftwaffe turned up according to plan. I had expected them to come down from the Vienna area and there they were ahead of us, preparing for a head-on attack.

But they weren't expecting escorting fighters out here, right over the target. They were at about 25,000ft., manoeuvering to come down on the leading box of bombers at about 20,000ft. That was why I'd come in at 30,000ft., to get the jump on them.

As radio call-sign for the whole Group, I had chosen "Horseback", borrowed from my Group in England. The call-sign for the Squadron was "Sunbeam". The other two were "Moonglow" and "Starlight". It was time to use them.

"Horseback leader here. Bandits at 10 o'clock are starting their attack. Sunbeam going down to head them off. Moonglow, give us cover, making sure there are none on your tail when you follow us down.

Starlight, give close cover to the rest of the bomber formations".

By the end of the message, I had rolled on my back and was screaming down vertically to get the speed we needed to catch up with them. We also had the sun behind us. It was a perfect interception. Curving in behind them put the section on my left directly on their tails. There were four of them, but my usual quick look behind confirmed what I suspected, there were more coming down behind.

"Horseback Leader to Sunbeam Red Three! Take your section in to attack! We'll cover you!"

"Sunbeam Red Three - Ah'm on mah way!"

It was Hogan.

They opened fire too soon, but the 109s were intent on their prey. I glanced behind again. About eight 109s were coming down on us. The other squadron was coming down too, but they were too far behind. It was time for us to turn into the 109s.

"Sunbeam Red Section, BREAK RIGHT!" I yelled, and racked the plane round in a tight upward turn. The 109s flashed by, continuing their dive instead of breaking into us. I rolled out of my tight turn and dived after them, checking that my flight was with me. Smitty was there on my wing, but Hogan and his wingman were still in a dive, hotly pursuing the first 109s. But the next gaggle of 109s was on their tails and gaining fast.

"Sunbeam Red Three, break right, you've got eight behind you! BREAK!" I shouted.

"Ah'm gonna get him! Ah'm gonna get him!" Hogan yelled.

"Not before they get you! I can't cover you unless you break!"

Hogan saw the 109 on his tail and started to break just as the German began firing. His wingman broke with him, but not hard enough. As it was, his turn wasn't tight enough to get enough deflection lead, but it allowed me to cut the corner by turning tighter. I slid underneath him and pulled up. I didn't need to aim; the 109 filled my windscreen.

At that range, you couldn't miss. I jammed on the rudder to avoid the debris from the stricken 109 and continued my turn to get onto the one on Hogan's tail.

I heard Hogan yell "Somebody get this bastard off my tail!"

"Just keep turning, Sunbeam Red Three. I'm nearly in range!"

I had to open fire before I was close enough, but it worked. He must have seen the tracers and then me and Smitty coming up. He flipped over on his back and dived for the deck. It was the old Luftwaffe evasive action, which had worked fine against Hurricanes, Spitfires and Russian fighters, but this boy didn't know that Mustangs had a slight edge on the Messerschmidt in the dive, and in this case I had more speed to start with. It took me only a few seconds to catch him and give him three bursts from close range. One of them must have hit the right wing root and the speed of the dive did the rest. The plane kept going. The wing fluttered and tumbled past me.

I zoomed back up. Smitty was still with me and Hogan and his wingman not far behind.

"Horseback Leader here! Sunbeam reforming at 6 o'clock to the bomber stream at angels 25,000. Moonglow, cover the bombers on their right, Starlight on their left!"

We'd broken up the head-on attack and the Germans wouldn't be able to get into position to mount another one. Any attacks now would come from the rear and the flanks.

Only a few minutes had elapsed since we first attacked and it was easy to re-assemble the squadron and get back up into position on the bombers. They were over the target now, but their problem was flak. It was light compared to Berlin and the Ruhr, but one B-24 took a hit and had to feather one engine.

As the bomber stream swung away from the target, the lame B-24 was able to keep up by cutting the corners, but as they started to straighten out for the long haul home, she started to lag behind. Finally, the gap was such that I was sure any German fighters following us would pounce on the last bomber.

"Horseback here! Sunbeam Red Three, take over the lead. I'm going back with my wingman to nurse that straggler!"

There was a pause, then Hogan drawled, "I reckon Starlight Leader can take over. I'll give you cover!"

"O.K." I said. "I guess two prima donnas are better than one!"

Almost as we turned back, a red flare curved out from the straggler. She was under attack already. I took my flight of four back over the straggler on the sun side. Two 109s were coming up behind the bomber. I flipped over and dived down vertically to get speed. We pulled out below and behind the Germans.

"Sunbeam Red Three, you take the one on the left. Sunbeam Red Two, take the one on the right. They haven't seen us, so don't open fire until the wingspan fills your windscreen. Take your time!"

I knew they wouldn't get close enough before opening fire, but range closed fast. Hogan got a definite hit. It went down flaming.

Smitty was bouncing around as he went in. Maybe he got in the slipstream. Maybe he was just too excited. He got hits, but the German broke hard right and Smitty slid past him. I was in just the right place and gave him a blast as he turned into my sights. It was an automatic reaction. I continued my turn and saw him spiralling down. Just as I was about to follow him, the canopy flew off and the pilot baled out.

We nursed the B-24 back to safety. Before leaving, I flew up close to see what damage they had sustained. I gave them the thumbs-up sign to indicate I thought they could make it. The two pilots were blowing kisses with both hands. In the side gun-bays, the gunners knelt down and salaamed like demented Muslims.

Back at base, there was wild excitement as pilots clamoured to tell their stories to the Intelligence Officer, or anyone else who would listen. Hogan and Smitty were waiting at my revetment when I taxied up and, as I congratulated them, the Intelligence Officer drove up.

"Did everybody get back?" I asked.

"Yessir! How did you do, Major? Any kills?"

"I may have knocked down a couple - and I can confirm one for Captain Hogan and one for Lieutenant Smith."

Before either of them could say anything, I told the Intelligence Officer, "Come with me - I have to 'phone General Bourne."

The General was so delighted, he insisted I fly straight to his HQ.

"I want to buy you a drink, Major, and so does Leon Johnson!"

After the drinks, General Bourne clapped me on the shoulder.

"You know, Major, when you asked to take that Group on a mission, I thought you were out of your mind. I'd had reports that the outfit was a mess. I even heard they were mutinous. I guess there really wasn't a problem, after all!"

"That's right, General."

"Well, I'm sorry to have dragged you down here, but we really appreciate it!"

"General," I said, "it was a pleasure!"

***

That was why the corporal and I were driving round the slums of Richmond, Virginia.

We finally stopped in front of a building which was even more broken down and derelict than the others.

"Well, sir," said the driver, "this is the street and this is the number!"

"I'll try it!" I said.

Reluctantly, and with disapproval expressed in his every gesture and movement, he got out and opened the door for me. Little black kids with enormous eyes followed me to the door. Even the porch of this building was gone, and the steps up to the front door were broken.

I turned to the kids. "You know where Mrs. Smith lives?"

They stared at me and said nothing.

I climbed the broken steps and went into a dark, smelly hallway. The first door I knocked on produced no answer, so I tried the one opposite. A large black woman in what had once been some sort of negligee finally opened the door. From her, at least I got a reaction.

Her eyes opened wide.

"What the hell do you want?"

"Does Mrs. Smith live here?"

"Elvira?"

"Yes," I said. "Mrs Elvira Smith."

She pointed upwards and closed the door on me. I began to climb the rickety wooden stairs, wishing I had never started on this thing. The state of the building deteriorated as I climbed higher, and when I got to the top floor I was ready to quit. After all, I had hardly known the guy.

I emerged through a hole in the floor into some sort of attic or garret. I could only stand upright in the middle, because of the sloping roof. There was a small door in front of me and one behind. I knocked on both of them and got no reply. Finally, I pushed one open and peered into a small dark area, which I took for a junk room. The floor was cluttered with piles of old clothes, china and a few pans and empty bottles. The only furniture seemed to be an old sink, a gas ring and a bed. On the bed sat a small black woman in an old-fashioned black dress.

"Mrs. Smith?" I asked.

"Yassah!"

"Did you get my letter?"

"Yassah!"

"I would have contacted you before, but I didn't get your son's letter until the war was over in Europe and I got out of prison camp."

There was no reply, so I struggled on.

"I brought his letter. I thought you might like to have it." I held it out to her. "It's a beautiful letter."

She stretched out a tentative hand and took it. She opened it, looked at it, but I could see she wasn't reading it.

"Would you like me to read it to you?"

She handed it back and I started to read.

"Dear Major Goodson,

I hope you don't mind me writing you. I am the black pilot who flew on your wing when you led the 999th group on their first mission to Wiener Neustadt. Maybe you don't even remember me, but I have never forgotten you. In fact, what you did and what you are has helped me every day. When I needed courage, I borrowed some of yours. When I didn't know what to do, I asked what you would do, and it showed me the way.

So you see, I owe you a lot.

I owe even more to one other person. In fact, I owe her everything, because she is my mother and everything she did was for me. I am enclosing her name and address in the hope that, if you get back to the States, you might see her. (She has no phone and doesn't read too good.) I think you could tell her better than I ever could that I know how much she has done for me and I love her for it.

I would not ask you to do this, but this letter will only be forwarded to you in the case of my death, and I hope you will understand.

Yours sincerely, Ashley Smith."

I gave it back to her and she clasped it in her hand.

Neither of us spoke. I looked around the sordid room and said lamely, "Is there anything I can do for you?"

"No, suh. Ah got mah pension." She followed my gaze. "Ah guess ah should fix this place up some - or maybe move out - but when my boy didn't come back, there didn't seem much point."

I nodded. "Well, if there is ever anything I can do, you know how to contact me."

She looked at me. "You mean that, suh?"

"Of course! Anything, anytime!"

"Well, suh, it's not just for me, it's for him too. This street ain't much, but it's where ah live. They're not bad folk, but they got no respect for me!"

"Oh, I'm sure they have!"

"No suh! They call me a broken-down, drunken ol' tramp. Well, that's O.K. But when I tell them my boy was a flying officer in the war, they call me a damn liar. I just want these bastards should know!"

There was a flash of defiance in the dark eyes.

"Of course!" I said. "I'll be glad to tell them!"

"No suh! Ah just want you to walk with me up this damn street. Ah just want to SHOW them! Then I can die happy!"

I helped her down the flights of wooden stairs and out into the street. I took her hand and put it under my arm and began the long, slow march, up one side of the street, down the other. Groups of wide-eyed children followed us. Men and women emerged from the houses and stared from windows and porches. She set the pace and established the solemnity of the occasion. She walked stiffly upright and looked neither to the right nor to the left.

After what seemed to me an agonisingly long time, we were back in front of her house. I stepped back and saluted.

"Goodbye," I said.

She looked up at me and raised her own hand in salute. In the other, she still clutched Smitty's letter. Two tears trickled slowly down her cheeks.

I stepped forward and took the frail little body in my arms. I felt her sobs and waited for them to die down. Then I bent and kissed her forehead. I took a folded handkerchief out of my pocket and gave it to her, but instead of wiping the tears from her face, she dabbed at the rows of ribbons on my chest, wet from her tears.

I took the handkerchief from her and dried her eyes and cheeks, turned on my heel and got into the car.

At the end of the street, I turned to look out of the window. The little figure was still standing outside the house. One hand was clasping the crumpled letter. The other was raised in a military salute.

I was dabbing at the tear-soaked ribbons when I caught the corporal looking at me in the rear-view mirror.

"Well, Corporal," I said, "now you know what war's all about. Tears on a row of medal ribbons!"

*****

Chapter 10

"THE LAST OF THE KNIGHTS"

They say that fighter pilots always look young. Maybe they're right. It was hard to believe that the war had been over for so many years. I looked at Bob Stanford-Tuck. He didn't look much different from the handsome young Wing-Commander I had first met at Duxford when 71 Eagle Squadron had been in his Wing. Doug Bader said, "Of course he looks the same - he still puts the same boot polish on his hair!"

But Doug, too, looked younger than his years, in spite of his grizzled grey hair; and his strength of character showed through more than ever. His pipe was clenched between his teeth and his jaw was thrown out as he forged ahead with his rolling gait, kicking his artificial legs forward.

Next to him was his old enemy, Adolf Galland, whose slicked-back hair and clipped moustache were as black as they had been when he was General in Command of the Fighter Command of the Luftwaffe.

It hadn't been easy to persuade Doug to accept the invitation to this re-union of German fighter pilots. I think the only thing that got him there was his respect for Galland, and his appreciation of the chivalrous treatment he had received from him when he was shot down and captured.

It was Galland who persuaded Goering to declare a truce to enable the RAF to bring over a leg to replace the one Bader had to leave behind when he baled out of his stricken Spitfire. The Luftwaffe plan, conveyed to the RAF by the Swedish Red Cross, was that a British Anson should land at Calais airfield, deliver the leg and take off again. Air-Vice Marshall Leigh Mallory was convinced it was a trap. Instead of a single aircraft, we came over with every fighter we could muster escorting a group of bombers.

It was weird. As we crossed the coast, there was none of the usual fierce flak. Over Northern France there was only perfect peace over the summer countryside. There was none of the usual clamour over the radio. Nothing. The silence was eerie.

Even over the airfield of St. Omer, there was none of the horrendous flak we had been used to. The bright flashes down below and the black smoke coming up were from our own bombs. Surely on the way home their fighters and flak would attack us. But no. It was a truce, and they'd given their word.

But although Doug had a grudging respect for Galland, there was none of the close friendship that existed between Galland and Tuck. Bader had given too much during the war and was too single-minded to change his convictions. For him, black and white, good and bad, were clear, and he knew which was which.

He made his position only too clear as we walked into the vast Munich Hofbrauhaus. As we stood at the top of the stairs and looked out over the hundreds of old fighter pilots, Bader said, "Christ! I never knew we left so many of the bastards alive!"

He hadn't said it to Galland, but Dolfo heard it. He smiled and said with his usual courtesy, "Most of these were on the Eastern Front. On the Western Front, you didn't leave many of us bastards alive!"

But a lot of the old 'bastards' were there. They had fought on every front from Spain to Russia, from the Arctic Circle to Africa. They had flown almost continuously from the first day of the war to the last. Just like us, they had heavy casualties, but if you survived long enough to develop the sort of sixth sense that only comes after many combat hours, your chances of survival got better and better.

I mentioned this to Jan Schild. "Yes," he said. "It was always the new ones. Towards the end, I never had time to get to know them before they were gone."

Jan was an old friend and enemy. Some years after the war, he tracked me down and came to see me. He reminded me of a dogfight over the Zuider Zee early in 1944. Schild was part of a Schwarm of FW-190s of III Gruppe of JG-26 under the command of Oberleutnant Karl Wilius.

They were climbing up to intercept US bombers when they were bounced by our fighters. During the melée, Schild was not able to prevent his C.O. from being shot down and killed, but he did see the identification letters VF-B on the attacking American plane.

When we met again after thirty years, I looked at him for a few moments. Once more, I saw my shots blasting into the 190 in front of me. Almost at the same moment, I sensed rather than saw the second

FW boring in to avenge his C.O. I racked my plane round into the attack, stomping top rudder with all my strength. The stream of shells and bullets passed underneath me as my plane side-slipped upwards and I hauled round in a desperate attempt to out-turn him and bring my guns to bear on him. But the P-47 Thunderbolt couldn't outmanoeuvre the brilliant Fw-190 at that low altitude and I couldn't get the better of its brilliant pilot. I was lucky to get home.

I wondered if Schild was thinking the same thing. I held out my hand. He came forward and grasped it. There was a moment's hesitation, then we were in a warm embrace.

Before he left, Jan took a small, square box from his pocket.

"I'd like you to have this," he said.

I opened it and saw on the background of velvet a silver wreath of leaves around a swooping eagle with outstretched wings. It was his Luftwaffe pilot's insignia, equivalent to our wings. With it was an inscription in German.

"To my brave and chivalrous adversary in 1941-1945 over England, France, Belgium, Holland and the Reich: Wing Com. James A. Goodson. Henrich Jan Schild, I & III/JG-26". *

He always used the nomenclature "Wing Commander." When I corrected him, he said, "Take it as a compliment. We know you got most of your victories and rank after you transferred to the American Air Force, but it means more to us that you fought in the earlier days with the British."

Gunther Rall agreed. "Yes, most of us would rate the British the better fighter pilots. That's nothing against the Americans, but we really didn't get a chance to evaluate them properly. When we were fighting the British, it was more of an equal fight and was often man to man. When the Americans came, they soon had us so out-numbered, we had to hit and run and couldn't stay to fight it out with them."

"Maybe that was true at the end of the war," I said. "But my 4th Fighter Group was out at the end of the bomber run over Berlin. We only had about 48 Mustangs against all the fighters the Luftwaffe could put up. We didn't often have you out-numbered then!"

* Now in the Library of the U.S. Air Force Academy, Colorado Springs.

"You're right! I was shot down myself over Berlin by an American fighter. Maybe it was you!"

"I doubt it," I said.

I looked at the handsome face with the charming smile. He looked at least ten years younger than his age (he still does!) and it was hard to believe that he had been shot down eight times, once breaking his back in three places. He was told he would probably never walk again and certainly would never fly again, but he defied all the laws of nature and the Luftwaffe to get back into combat and resume the contest to become the leading fighter pilot. At the end of the war, in succession to Hermann, he was Commander of JG-300, the Rammkommando, whose pilots were trained to bring down US four-engined bombers by ramming them; some years later, he became Commanding General of the new Luftwaffe.

The great Hofbrauhaus was filled with individual tables. Each table bore the number of a squadron, so that the survivors could be together.

All the names were there: JG-26 Schlageter, JG-2 Richtofen, JG-1 Oesau, JG-3 Udet, JG-5 Eismeer, JG-51 Hoeldens, JG-54 Grunherz, which built up a reputation on the Eastern Front under its great Kommodor Trautloft equal to that of JG-52 under Kommodores Hrabak and Graf, which at one time or another included such aces as Steinhoff, Hartmann, Barkhorn, Rall, Batz, Krupinski, Lipfert and Obleser - ten pilots who together accounted for 2205 enemy aircraft destroyed.

Among the large tables thronged with old comrades was one at which a white-haired, bearded, dignified figure sat alone. Hajo Hermann began his career in the Luftwaffe in 1935, and played a leading role as a bomber pilot in Spain with the Condor Legion, in the invasion of Poland, in the occupation of Norway, in the invasion of Holland, Belgium and France. He served throughout the Battle of Britain, and went from North Africa, Greece, Italy and Malta to the polar regions of Jan Mayen, Spitzbergen and Nova Zembla.

It was Herrmann who took a hand in the defence of Germany when the situation got really bad, and persuaded Goering to back his desperate plan. Hamburg had been virtually destroyed by RAF night bombing attacks which turned the centre of the city into a fiery blast furnace. The German night-fighter force depended on a complicated system of radar stations on the ground co-operating with airborne radar in Me-110s, Me-210s and JU-88s. This system guided the fighters onto the bombers as they approached the target, and again on their way home. Over the target city itself, defence was left entirely to the flak batteries, assisted by searchlights, but this was not very effective. The only real successes they had were from the night-fighters guided by radar, and from them the RAF Bomber Command began taking unacceptable losses.

But Germany's radar system was rendered completely impotent and the cities and their populations defenceless not by some great technological breaththrough, but simply by each bomber throwing out "chaff" - metal foil which disrupted the German radar and left both ground stations and fighters not just blind, but commpletely confused.

Searchlights and flak were all that was left to defend the cities of the Reich, and although the anxious citizens and the frustrated defence services saw the bombers held in the beams of the searchlights, they seldom saw the flak score a hit.

The Luftwaffe had accepted the myth that instrument flying was too difficult for single-engined fighters, so bad weather and night-flying was left to the bombers and twin-engined fighters. Hermann, though, remembered the Hurricanes and Spitfires during the Battle of Britain coming up against the German bombers at night, and even chasing them back to their bases and shooting them down in their landing patterns. He also knew that our Thunderbolts and Mustangs frequently climbed through 25,000ft. of cloud to escort our bombers when the German fighters were grounded by bad weather.

He may not have known that we had the great advantage of being able to practice our blind flying on the ground. The Link trainer, which simulated the flight of an aircraft, saved hundreds of planes and pilots. But as an experienced pilot who had flown every kind of fighter plane, Hermann knew that, though night-flying in a single-engined plane was more difficult and dangerous, it was perfectly practical.

He couldn't watch the destruction of the cities and the havoc of the fire-storms without doing something, and now he went straight to the top. Normally, he might not have got a hearing, but he found Herman Goering a broken man. For some time, he had been blamed by the German people for their defencelessness, and now he was feeling the wrath of Adolf Hitler too. When Hajo Herrmann came to him with his dramatic plan, he clutched at it.

It was drastic but simple and had the advantage, not of replacing existing defences, but of adding to them. The radar-directed twin-engined night fighters would continue to do their best against the bombers approaching and leaving the target; the flak would continue to operate over the cities; but they would work in close co-operation with Hermann, and the searchlights would be in even closer contact.

Realising that the RAF's navigational aids enabled them to locate their targets regardless of blackouts, Hermann called for maximum light over the target. All he asked for was a flak-free area above 18,000ft. and the help of the searchlights in catching and holding the bombers in their glare.

To discover when and where the bombers were going to hit, Hermann equipped his fighters with droppable fuel tanks to enable them to stay up over two hours and cover most of the north of Germany. Even when only ten planes were available, he insisted they be sent into action.

Before either the flak or the searchlights had been briefed on the new night-flyer force, a bomber force thought to be heading for the Ruhr turned south and hit Cologne. Hermann didn't hesitate. He led his little band into the battle over Cologne, into the glare of the searchlights, into the exploding flak, into the mass of bombers.

The ten fighters lived up to the name they had chosen, The Wild Boars. They charged into the fray, through the maelstrom of vivid flashes and sudden blackness, pouncing on the big bombers. They destroyed twelve, for the loss of one fighter.

The Wild Boars were criticised by day and night fighters alike, but for Goering it was the only hope of stopping the fire-storm raids. He gave Hermann the green light to form a full Geschwader of single-engined night fighters and JG-300 was born.

At the end of August 1943, RAF Bomber Command began hitting Berlin with the same fire-storm tactics that had destroyed Hamburg. On the night of August 24th, the Wild Boars, backed by other night fighters using the same tactics, shot down 56 bombers; on September 1st they shot down 47 and on September 4th, another 26, causing the RAF to withdraw from the destruction of Berlin for the time being. They waited for the worsening autumn weather to give them better protection from the Wild Boars in the air, and make take-offs and landings and navigation more difficult for the still relatively inexperienced German pilots.

So, after their moments of glory, the Wild Boars faded out of the picture. They hadn't saved Germany. They hadn't saved Hamburg or Berlin. But they had given the German radar experts time to develop a counter-measure to the British chaff. They gave an answer to those who asked, "Where is the Luftwaffe?" Hermann, who had been promoted by Goering to report directly to him, was relegated to relative obscurity - until the next time.

The next time came towards the end of the war. By now, the greatest threat was the American daylight bomber offensive. Germany had the answer - the Me262 jet fighter; but they needed to buy time until they could build enough of them to knock the Fortresses out of the sky.

Again, Hermann came up with a drastic solution. In their aggressive attacks on the night bombers, the Wild Boars had sometimes collided with them. Sometimes the pilots survived. The bombers didn't. If the bombing offensive could be slowed down until a hundred jet fighters were ready, most of the 109s and 190s would be obsolete. It was therefore not senseless bravado, but a logical conclusion, that JG-300 should carry their aggressive tactics one step further, and actually ram the bombers.

This solution was drastic even for Goering. He finally agreed, on condition that only volunteers should be involved, probably believing that, with no hope of winning the war, some of the pilots just might volunteer. Ninety-five per cent of them did.

But it was too late. Hermann and what was left of his units finally found themselves squeezed between the Americans, the Russians, the British and Tito's partisans. Berlin and most of Germany were in Allied hands; Hitler was dead; Doenitz was on the point of surrender. It was time for Hermann to do the same.

He felt responsible for those in his command. He knew, and deeply resented, the British and American response which had probably greatly prolonged the war - Unconditional Surrender. He sent three men to sound out the Russians. One came back. The others were held hostage and under threat of death unless Herrmann himself came to them.

Like Hartmann, Graf and many other German officers, his loyalty was to his men. Once more, he took off in his Fieseler Storch. He could have flown to Switzerland, or anywhere. He flew to his men and ten years as a prisoner in Russian prison camps.

When he finally came back, it was to a new world. It was a world which had forgotten Hajo Hermann and didn't want to know about him or the war. He had only his indomitable will - which had survived everything the NKVD could throw at him - and the support of his loyal family. With their help, he began a new life, studying law and finally practising it with the same success he had achieved in everything he had undertaken.

When that career came to an end, he wrote a book about his career as a flyer. It is written as he speaks, blunt, straight, with no apologies, no complaints, just the way it was, the story of the Luftwaffe, the story of Hajo Herrmann.*

The book stops when he goes into the Russian concentration camps. He talks about other things, but never that. And I wasn't about to ask him about the camps. But he spoke of other things, of his reaction when he attended the trial of some of those involved in the attempt to assassinate Hitler.

"I couldn't understand why these men, who were opposed to the system, didn't take advantage of the great forum of the crowded court-room to express themselves more strongly and decisively. If I went into the session fearing I would see the authority of Adolf Hitler seriously shaken, I came out with the feeling that we must go on with him - what else could we do? Unconditional Surrender? No!

"I realised that the defendants were criticising the political system, copying the enemy broadcasts. Occasionally I had listened to them myself. The Allies pretended it was all about doing away with the system and the overthrow of Hitler. I found this boring, a repetition of 1914/18; get rid of the monarchy and chase the Kaiser out! When that was done, they took our colonies, our markets, mines and money. We weren't going to let it happen this time.

"We weren't fighting for a Fuehrer or a system, but as German soldiers for Germany, even if it became more and more entangled in difficulties. What did Nazi slogans mean to me? I'm sure Marxism meant no more to the Russians. Their Fatherland meant far more to them."

Not all the great surviving Luftwaffe heroes were there in the Hofbrauhaus. Many felt they had given their all for their country and

(* Bewegtes Leben", Hajo Herrmann, Motorbuch Verlay,Stuttgart)

received nothing but undeserved criticism in return. They had seen all their efforts and sacrifice wasted by the stupidity of others, so they had wiped the slate clean and started new careers and closed out the past.

One of those was Helmut Lipfert. He wasn't there, but I knew where he was. We had first met at 30,000ft. over Germany in early 1944.

As my Group of Mustangs took over the escort of some 300 Fortresses and Liberators just before they started their bombing run, we saw nine Me109s up ahead of the bombers. When their leader took them down in a head-on attack, I led two flights down to head them off. They must have seen us, but they continued their attack until they were hurtling through the mass of bombers, with us in close pursuit.

Then we were through. We had got two of them, but there were still seven left. Instead of continuing their dive and heading for home, their leader racked his plane round to lead an attack from the side on a lower formation of bombers. This time, we were able to cut the corner on them and when they broke off their attack, there were only three of them.

Once more, they swung round and attacked the last box of bombers. Once more, we attacked them. We got one more of them, but I couldn't catch the leader and his wingman before they attacked two straggling Liberators. I was gaining on them, but when I opened fire I ran out of ammunition.

The two remaining 109s must also have been out of ammunition. They broke off their attack on the bombers, but the two Liberators were going down. The leader must have known I had no ammo left, or perhaps was just confident that he could out-turn me. In any case, he didn't bother to tighten his turn as I came up beside him and saw the markings on his plane. I waved. He waved back.

It took me many years to trace him. I first learned that his squadron was the great JG-52 and then, much later, that the leader on that day had been Helmut Lipfert, who had chalked up over 200 victories on the Russian front. Finding him was much more difficult.

The trail finally led me to a village near Cologne. The Post Office directed me to the school. He was the schoolmaster.

He remembered the mission well, but with sadness.

"We lost too many pilots that day," he said.

"Yes, but how many bombers did you knock down?" I asked.

"I claimed one Liberator and my wingman another."

"But what about the others? They must have scored?"

He shrugged. "There was no-one to claim them and no-one to confirm them."

I looked around at the happy schoolchildren.

"Do these kids and their parents know you were one of the leading fighter aces of the war?"

He smiled. "I hope not!"

Then, after a pause, he added, "But I hope they think I'm a good schoolteacher!"

Helmut Lipfert had his priorities right.

Many of the Luftwaffe pilots I met after the war were remarkable men. For five years, they had clambered into their 109s and 190s and taken off to do battle, just as we had, yet for four of those years on the Western Front they had been more hopelessly outnumbered than any fighting force in history. When Germany invaded Russia at the end of the Battle of Britain, only two squadrons, JG-26 Schlageter and JG-2 H Richthofen, were left on the Western Front to try to stem the growing might of the RAF and the USAAF.

When half a million Allied troops, covered by five thousand planes, invaded Normandy, only part of JG-26 was available and only two pilots, Pips Priller and his wingman, were able to penetrate the protective ring of Allied fighters and appear over the beachhead. Ignoring the thousands of aircraft above and around them, dodging the massive fire from the ground, they strafed the equipment moving across the beaches until they ran out of ammunition and then somehow escaped back to base.

But they were used to attacking overwhelming odds. How often over Berlin and other German cities had we pursued a handful of Luftwaffe fighters in head-on attacks on the bomber fleets, shot some down, followed them in their headlong dive through the masses of bombers, only to see those that were left turn back and attack again and again.

And during those years of unrelenting, constant combat, whilst their toughest enemies would confirm that they maintained the highest standards of chivalry and heroism, their own High Command kept them desperately short of the equipment they needed and constantly blamed them for the tragic results of the decisions that were inflicted on them by everyone from Hitler downwards.

No-one was more frustrated than Adolf Galland. As General of the Luftwaffe Fighter Command, he was undoubtedly the greatest expert on fighter tactics on either side. He, more than anyone, knew the importance of building up the fighter arm to stop the bomber fleets he knew the Allies would be sending against Germany, and which eventually destroyed the Nazi's production capacity.

The story of the Me-262 jet fighter was typical. When Galland saw the prototype flying, he saw at once that this revolutionary plane, for which the Allies had no counter-measure, would probably give Germany its only chance of winning the war. Imagine his disbelief when Hitler decreed that it was to be developed only as a bomber, and not as a fighter.

Galland fought so hard for the strategy that he knew to be right that he made many enemies in high places, but this did not deter him.

As a last resort, when Goering continued to thwart him, he demanded a meeting with Hitler. The Air Marshall reluctantly agreed and Galland finally found himself able to present his arguments to the Fuehrer himself.

Even when Hitler cut him off, Galland returned to the attack until Hitler went into one of his hysterical monologues when it was impossible to talk to him. But Galland had at least been more courageous than Goering and Milch in confronting the Fuehrer.

The result was that he was dismissed from his position and remained in disgrace until the war was nearing its end.

Finally, when it was too late, the High Command tacitly admitted that they had been wrong and Galland and his squadron commanders had been right. They finally gave priority to building up the strength of the fighter arm and even allowed the first and only jet-powered aircraft, the Me262, to be used in the fighter role for which it was designed, instead of as a bomber attempting to carry out "revenge" attacks, which served no purpose other than to feed Goebbel's propaganda and Hitler's ego.

The great General Galland was brought back, not to head the German Fighter Command once more, but to lead a squadron. Ironically, he now got the plane he had fought for, and for which he had sacrificed his career.

They came from all over, the last surviving Luftwaffe aces, to join his squadron, JV-44. Luetzow came up from Italy; Barkhorn, Krupinski, Hohagen and Schell left hospital beds where they were lying wounded. They brought with them their experience. Many had fought in Spain, most had started their scoring records in the Battle of Britain. They brought with them their rank, their fame, their victories and the highest decorations the Third Reich could bestow.

Those top-ranking aces who didn't come were the ones who couldn't come. They were either fighting for their lives on the Eastern Front, or prisoners of war, or dead. Those that did come didn't come because they were ordered to; most came against orders. They didn't come with any hope of staving off the inevitable defeat; it was too late for that. They didn't come out of loyalty to the Fuehrer who had consistently let them down, or to the National Socialists; their oath as Luftwaffe officers had always prevented them from joining any political party, even if they had the time and the inclination, which they didn't.

They came to join their friends in the last great "Fliegerei". This was the Squadron of the Experts.

Thanks to the superiority of the Me262 jet and its great pilots, JV-44 had more to fear on the ground than in the air. Their base at Riem, near Munich, was constantly under an umbrella of hostile fighters and bombers. Take-offs and landings were suicidal. The pilot had to give his attention to flying a highly technical piece of machinery, keep a sharp look-out for enemy fighters diving down on him, and somehow find a take-off path through the craters left by the latest raid, only some of which had been hastily filled in.

On April 18, 1945, "Macky" Steinhoff came to grief, after flying one thousand combat missions since 1939. He was taking off with full tanks, with an extra load of rockets under the wings, when one wheel caught in a newly filled-in bomb crater. The plane swung, the undercarriage collapsed and the plane crashed at close to 200 mph in a blast of flame. Not even Steinhoff can understand how he managed to get out in the few seconds between the crash and the explosion. But he survived, though the burns which destroyed the fine features of his face meant that never again would he be the handsomest officer in the Luftwaffe. It is a measure of his courage and ability that he went on to become Chief of Staff of the NATO Air Force in Central Europe and finally, in 1966, Commander (Inspector) of the German Air Force.

On the day the American and Soviet armies met on the Elbe and as Berlin and Vienna fell, Galland called together his band and told them, "Militarily speaking, the war is over. Even our action cannot change anything...I shall continue to fight...because I am proud to belong to the last fighter pilots of the German Luftwaffe. Only those who feel the same should go on fighting with me."

They all did.

The day after, Galland joined Steinhoff in hospital, having been shot up by Mustangs, but managing to land his battered plane at Riem whilst it was still under intensive attack by bombers and fighters.

Heinz Baer took over the squadron, but as the American forces were now in Munich, they had to leave Riem. At Salzburg, the remaining Me262s were lined up. Allied fighters circled overhead, but did not attack. They knew the Germans had no fuel and they could see the American tanks rattling towards the airfield. The beautiful powerful jets, with their modern rocket weaponry, so far in advance of anything the Allies had, would soon fall into their hands.

The last Luftwaffe fighter pilots had offered to turn their planes over intact to the Allies in return for a few concessions, but the answer came back: Unconditional Surrender.

They looked up at the circling Mustangs. They looked towards the perimeter of the airfield where they could already hear the clanking and roar of the American tanks.

There comes a time when the kindest thing a cavalryman can do for his beloved charger is to take out his service pistol and deliver the 'coup de grace'.

As the first American tank appeared on the Salzburg airfield, the first Me262 exploded in a burst of flame. It was followed by one after another, until all that was left of the beautiful sleek jets was their funeral pyre.

It was May 3rd, 1945. For JV-44, the war was over.

For others, it was not.

On May 8th, two Me109s took off from the improvised landing strip at Deutsch Brod in Czechoslovakia. Almost immediately, they were over the town, where a rising pall of smoke and the columns of infantry and tanks confirmed to the two German fighters that the town had fallen to the rapidly-advancing Russian army. From this altitude, they could also see a number of YAK-11s covering the advance.

Just as he had done hundreds of times during the last two and a half years, the leading 109 of the Rotte manoeuvred into position, signalled his wingman with a flick of his wing, and rolled into the dive. He pulled out to come up behind one of the YAKs, waited until the Russian plane almost filled his windscreen, pressed the firing button and slid away to avoid colliding with his stricken victim.

Major Erich Hartmann had scored his 352nd, and last, victory.

He was used to scoring at least twice on a mission, but as he zoomed up again to position himself for another attack, that sixth sense which all veteran fighter pilots develop caused him to look up into the sun. There, the flashes of sunlight on silver fuselages told that Mustangs of the USAAF were coming down, scouring the area for the last survivors of the Luftwaffe.

What Hartmann had seen on the ground was now confirmed in the air; the Western Front and the Eastern Front had met and there was no retreat possible for the Luftwaffe, and no way to go on fighting.

Hartmann dodged the American and Russian fighters by diving down through the smoke pall hanging over the burning town. His last view of the enemy was of the Mustangs and YAKs overhead.

Back at base, he clambered out of "Karaya-One" (Sweetheart one),which bore a bleeding heart insignia pierced by an arrow and the name of his new young wife, Ursel. His faithful friend and mechanic, Bimmel, who had once tramped miles behind the Russian lines to look for Hartmann when he didn't return from a mission, was automatically starting the drill for immediate re-fuelling and re-arming.

Hartmann looked at him steadily. The shake of his head was almost imperceptible, but Bimmel understood.

We all thought of German officers as being extremely conscious of rank and anything but democratic as Americans understood the term, but I never found any trace of this among Luftwaffe officers. When Laddie Lucas asked Gunther Rall to write about the most unforgettable character he had ever met, Rall didn't write about the great generals who were his peers and friends; he wrote about a sergeant-pilot. In the case of Hartmann, when he was asked about the man who had been his greatest friend and inspiration, he didn't hesitate. It was Bimmel.

Lt.Col. Hermann Graf, his Kommodore, handed Hartmann a radio message as he came in to report. It read:

GRAF AND HARTMANN BOTH FLY IMMEDIATELY TO DORTMUND AND SURRENDER TO BRITISH FORCES. ALL OTHER JG-52 PERSONNEL WILL SURRENDER AT DEUTSCH BROD TO SOVIET FORCES. GENERAL SEIDEMANN. AIR FLEET COMMANDER.

Hartmann looked at his Kommodore for orders.

"Bubi", Graf began.

It was Krupinksi who first called Hartmann "Bubi" when Erich first joined the squadron and flew on the colourful old veteran's tail. The name "Kid" stuck with him. Now, with his blonde hair, blue eyes and open boyish face, he still looked more like a teenager than the Major commanding No. 1 Gruppe of JG-52, veteran of over 1500 missions. In fact, he had just turned 23.

"Bubi, the General knows that if you or I fall into Russian hands, we'll never be heard of again. Between us, we've shot down 350 Russian planes and, if that's not enough, the fact that we both wear the Diamonds will clinch it."

Graf moved to the flap of the tent and looked out at the crowd of two thousand men, women and children who were anxiously looking towards him. They were the personnel of JG-52 and their families. There were also refugees of many nationalities, including Russians, fleeing from the Red Army. They all knew what awaited them if they fell into the hands of that Army; they had seen it with their own eyes. Bubi Hartmann and Hermann Graf knew, too.

"Bubi, you don't think I could jump into a plane and leave all these defenceless?"

"No, sir, I agree."

Hartmann immediately arranged for the destruction of the planes, starting with Karaya One. Graf started organising the evacuation of his people. The plan was to march the entire convoy to the West to surrender to the American army. Their advance units were reported to be only a few miles away.

In fact, tanks of the US 16th Armoured Division were forging ahead well into Czechoslovakia, and it was they and the 90th Infantry Division who accepted the formal surrender of Graf and Hartmann.

The Germans were surprised when the GIs took not only their weapons, but also their watches and other personal belongings as "souvenirs", including Hartmann's logbooks and photograph collection, which were never recovered. But the Germans took it all fairly philsophically. These were small indignities compared to the treatment they could have expected from the Russians.

The only thing that mattered was that the American officers had given their word that the Germans would not be turned over to the Russians.

They were loaded into trucks and transported to the area liberated by the Americans. There, they were interned in a large open-air encampment, which soon became overcrowded with thousands of surrendering soldiers and refugees.

There was no food, no shelter, no sanitation. Many took advantage of the confusion to escape and make their way towards the west. They knew what happened to Germans caught by the Russians, whether they were ex-soldiers, old men, women or children and they wanted to get as far away as possible.

Graf and Hartmann, however, had been given the responsibility of maintaining discipline among their charges and, as good officers, they did so; they were also convinced that it was in the best interests of their people to keep them all together.

Even when they were separated from the others and herded into trucks again, they accepted the Americans' assurance that they were being taken to the west, to Regensburg, for proper processing. It was only when the trucks stopped and they were ordered out that the terrible truth began to dawn on them. They were standing in a large field, entirely surrounded by soldiers of the Red Army.

The peaceful meadows were immediately transformed into a kaleidoscope of horror scenes.

The men were separated from the women, the boys from the girls. The men found themselves with rifles and machineguns in their stomachs. The women and girls were subjected to the worst imaginable tortures, or rape and debauchery.

The sergeant's wife was weeping, begging them to take her and spare her 12 year old daughter. She was kicked in the stomach and shot through the head. Her murderer then turned to join the others in the multiple rape of the child. The men had to watch as the ravished girl finally crawled towards them and collapsed. They watched and listened for an hour as the whimpering gradually faded and she died.

Men struggling to free themselves in an attempt to stop the slaughter were shot down. Ace pilots wept openly. Russian soldiers, their uniforms covered with the blood of their victims, staggered back to relieve their comrades who had been restraining the men, so that they too could join in the carnage.

And the Americans? When the orgy started, they seemed stunned. Their orders had been to turn the Germans over to the Russians. This they had done. There were no orders to cover what was happening now. They did nothing until two young German girls, already stripped naked, ran to the American trucks and tried to clamber aboard. The GIs hauled the weeping children up to safety. Furious, some of the Russians began shooting in the direction of the trucks, whilst others started to move menacingly towards them. The Army started up its trucks and left.

The ravaging, brutality and murder went on throughout the night. Finally, one by one, like rag dolls, the women and children were thrown back to their menfolk.

The scene the next morning was, if possible, even more gruesome. Inside the ring made by the tanks, many of the bodies did not move. The men had stabbed or suffocated their half-dead, ravished wives and daughters, then committed suicide.

Similar scenes were being enacted throughout East Germany, whipped up by the campaign of hatred and vengeance launched by the Soviet government and given form and voice by Ilya Ehrenburg. But the rising flood of disgust as news of the atrocities leaked out caused the Soviets to order their generals to bring the troops under control.

The day after the nightmare of JG-52, a Russian general appeared with his staff and new orders were given. The scene was now quiet. In addition to the corpses left from the rape, murder and suicide of the Germans, the bodies of three Russian soldiers, who had raped a young girl after the order to stop had been given, swung from a gibbet for all to see. The General had no further trouble. His men understood him.

The fate of most of the German survivors is unknown, but Bubi Hartmann, together with Graf and other leading Luftwaffe pilots, were shipped off to Russian prison camp. There, as "war criminals", they were subjected to torture, solitary confinement, starvation, disease and brain-washing.

Hartmann was once led to beg his NKVD captors for a gun and bullets to let him end his life, but he probably wouldn't have done it even if they had been given to him. The one thing which sustained him was the love of his young wife, who had promised to wait for him, for one year, for twentyfive years, or for ever.

When a gaunt Hartmann came back from ten and a half years of hell, she was there, waiting.

Of course, many of the great aces didn't survive the war, but one of the greatest commanders, Pips Priller, fought all through it and rebuilt his life afterwards to become the successful manager of the Rigele Brewery in Augsburg, which is where I met him, only to die of a heart attack in 1961 at the age of 45.

The veterans of JG-26 "Schlageter" Squadron still call themselves "Schlagertraner". Jan Schild was one of them. One of the first questions he asked me was "Did you know Pips Priller?"

I remember Pips Priller as one of the most charming men I have ever met. Unlike many Germans, his politeness was not stiff or unnatural, but a reflection of his essential niceness. I once asked Jan Schild if, under pressure, Priller's charm had ever cracked.

"Never!" said Jan. "It wasn't a veneer - it was him. He wasn't just a great Kommodore, he was a nice guy!"

The Schlageteraners rated him with the great, but with a difference. Jan said, "We revered Moelders, we honoured Galland, we loved Pips Priller."

I've never heard Moelders referred to as "Werner", and I've only heard his closest friends and the Americans and British call Galland "Dolfo"; but nearly everyone who knew Priller called him "Pips".

This German nickname - something akin to "Shorty" - referred to his height of 5ft.4in., not really a worthy sobriquet for the Kommodore of JG-26 and then Inspector of Day Fighters West; holder of the Knights Cross to the Iron Cross with Oak Leaves and with Swords; but with Pips it was somehow the greatest tribute of all that his friends, great and small, could call him that. To them - and, I think, to him - it meant more than having the 'Swords'.

To me, Priller was more than polite and charming. He asked many questions and gave the impression that he was intensely interested in my replies. He wanted to know how I was treated in prison camp.

"Well," I said, "the Luftwaffe were tough, but correct. Of course, we were supposed to get the same food as German soldiers and that was obviously not the case; but they knew we got Red Cross parcels and no-one starved to death. No, the problems started when we were outside the control of the Luftwaffe. The fifty RAF officers who were shot in the Great Escape were shot by the Gestapo."

Pips responded easily, "It's always the politicians, not the military, that are guilty of war crimes. In every country, it's the same."

"Yes," I said, "there were two Germanies during the war - the Nazis and the non-Nazis."

"That's what I'm saying!" he said. "The politicians and those who were not politicians. As officers, as you know, we were not allowed to have political affiliations."

"And what about the mass of ordinary Germans, the man and woman in the street?"

The warm smile faded, and a look of infinite sadness and sympathy clouded the handsome face.

"That was the greatest treachery of all time! Those decent, honest, patriotic people who sacrificed their homes, their loved ones, their everything, without complaint, because they believed. They believed all the lies. So in the end, they not only lost their homes and belongings - that's nothing. But they lost their husbands, wives, sons, daughters; though even that, one can get over; but to lose your dreams, your faith, your everything, that they didn't deserve. The politicians! I'll never forgive them for that! Nor the ones who caused so many to lose their freedom!"

I felt sure he was thinking of Hartmann, Hermann and the hundreds of German airmen, soldiers and sailors who had suffered for years in Russian camps for no other crime than having fought with outstanding bravery for their country. What I didn't know then was that he was also thinking of his own many months of captivity when the war was over when, like Galland and many other high-ranking German officers, he was held in captivity by the British.

Without any evidence, he was accused of shooting down a British plane, seeing the pilot bale out, returning to base, landing, driving to where the pilot was sitting by the road, pulling out a revolver and shooting him in the back. Priller's log-book showed that, on the day in question, he had neither taken off from nor landed at that base. But although his log-book was lying on the table, he was not allowed to refer to it. He was supposed to be able to remember from which airfield he had taken off on one particular day, having taken off some 1300 times during his career. He was threatened with hanging and was probably saved only by a providential change, the replacement of his interrogator.

The self-righteous politicians (an RAF friend of mine called them, crudely but aptly, "the barnacles on the arsehole of victory") who crept out of the woodwork when the war was over never asked those of us who had fought the Luftwaffe what we thought of our adversaries. If they had, we would have told them that you could never accuse the great German Kommodres of lack of chivalry. Moelders was fanatical about fairness and honour. Priller himself had a pilot court-martialled for attacking a train in England.

Yet they knew that the Allied fighters regularly attacked passenger trains and even shot German pilots who baled out. One of Lipfert's boys was shot in his parachute and Rudi Simmer told me that, when he was shot down, two Mustangs strafed him as he ran across a field when he landed.

"They must have been from one of the new squadrons," I said.

"They had red noses!"

I didn't reply.

I asked Priller if he was aware that his politicians didn't maintain the same high standards.

"If I had known," he said, "I would have felt it was all the more necessary for us to keep our standards of decency. They may have believed that the ends justified the means. I never did."

I asked him why, when the war was obviously lost, he kept on fighting against hopeless odds.

"What were you fighting for? Not for Hitler. Not for victory; it was impossible. Not for Germany; Germany was finished."

"First, for my boys, my squadron. They were looking to me and I couldn't let them down."

It was the answer that Hartmann and Herrman had given and for which they suffered ten years of Russian captivity without complaint.

"Secondly, if I only shot down one bomber, I saved the lives of those it could have killed. And partly, I had to live with myself."

I nodded. "This above all, to thine own self be true, and it must follow as the night the day, thou canst not then be false to any man."

The smile was back again.

"You see! You understand! Why did you ask?"

Yes, Pips, I understood.

Yes, Jan, I knew Pips Priller.

Galland put it another way when he stood up to deliver his speech at the final dinner of the re-union.

He looked out over the Luftwaffe pilots who had followed him with devotion, over the Spaniards who had fought with him from the very beginning, over the Hungarians, Italians, Rumanians and the rest; over the British, Americans, Czechs and Poles who had fought him, sometimes with hatred and sometimes with fear, but always with respect. Slowly, he raised his glass.

"Gentlemen, we have with us tonight men of many nationalities who have fought on different sides, but we have one thing in common: we fought for our country with courage, sincerity and chivalry.

"Gentlemen, to you! You were the last of the Knights!"

*****